Sad is not bad. But us grief virgins often struggle with feeling like sad IS bad, which makes us try to hide all the feels (especially at Church). But imagine if sad was safe (especially at Church). Don't paralyze your feelings. Instead, feel all the dang feels, and discover that loss doesn't have the last word. I love Jesus a lot and I cuss a little. I'm a deep feeler and a daring thinker. I believe we must face the ungood to find the good. And when we do, **I promise we'll find Life from Loss.**

- brooke mardell

Let's be honest. No one *wants* to grieve. Yet loss and grief are some of the few guarantees we get in this broken world. Still, we are often surprised by them. Unprepared. *Grief virgins.* With no idea what to do when Sad enters our story.

Sad comes in all shapes and sizes, and usually meets us at the intersection of Ideal and Real ... Broken Promises. Neglect. Cancer. Heart attack. Death. Disability. Infertillity. Unemployment. Empty seats at the Thanksgiving table. Moving. Loss of a dream.

And loss can make us feel ... well, lost. Our Sad can be paralyzing, crippling, terrifying.

But our Sad can also be Sacred.
It can reveal who we really are, and who God really is.

That's why this Bible Study exists. Because the God of the Bible is near to the broken-hearted. Jesus is a man acquainted with sorrow. And before it was 'good', the fateful Friday that he hung on a tree was the greatest grief yet known.

And while Sad is passive, Grief is active. Grief is a shifting, moving, dynamic *response* to whatever has broken our heart. It is the working out of what has crept in. It is a storm. It can move fast or slow. Its winds can be gentle or fierce. It always brings rain.

The work of *Friday's Rain* is to wash away the facades, the pretenses, the illusions, and reveal to us what is most true: we are deeply loved, by a wild Belover.

This study was born from a broken heart as I faced my First Great Grief – my first '*Friday*': unexplained infertility. As a Grief Virgin, I didn't know what to do as an internal storm exposed my heart in its rawest form. But in following the footsteps of others entrusted with loss, I found a God more wild and tender and unpredictable and loving and fierce and GOOD than I could have imagined. This study is not designed to stifle our feels nor to dwell in them, but to bring them out of hiding and brave the Sad-storm-of-Grief, daring to feel all the drops of rain as they fall.

You may not be in a specific season of grief right this moment, but chances are that you have been, or someone you love is - and let's be real, this world gives us a new reason to grieve every day. So whether it's a past or present pain you carry, your own or that of someone you love, God has something to say – about you, and about Him.

And you just might be surprised at what the rain reveals.

TABLE OF CONTENTS

Use this study for how it works for YOU. It's set up to allow for 5 days/week of study for 6 weeks. But hear me here: **it's you and Jesus time**, so don't let something like numbers on a page dictate when, where or how you study.

Each day to go through a part of the grief-storm.

- The *lightning strike*: the grief that rocks them.
- The *thunder*: God's ask. The sacred invitation *into* the storm.
- The *storm gear*: what will be required of them as they gear up.
- The *path*: how the storm plays out.
- The *cloudbreak*: what is revealed after the storm.

Grief brings two big questions to the table: who am I, and who is God? Really, most of Scripture's stories are about this. We will look at five of them. In hearing their stories, we will find our own. **We will find what's revealed after Friday's rain ...**

Unless otherwise noted, I am using the ESV (English Standard Version) as my reference point. I also paraphrase a lot. Go with it. This study is written from an evangelical, protestant Christian perspective. You don't have to share this perspective to share in this Study. Just know that I am writing as one who believes in a vibrant and intimate relationship with the God of the Bible through the saving work of Jesus as the Christ. If you want to talk more about what I mean, email me at brooke@brookemardell.com

MOSES – Day 1
The lightning strike: Egypt, Slavery, Murder, Rejection

Meet Moses ...

... Just about everyone knows Moses. Thank you, Charlton Heston. The Ten Commandments, the parting of the Red Sea. Epic battles won. And a few lost. The man who so bravely followed God into and through the wilderness (I said bravely, not perfectly), and upon whom God's glory shown.

Before there was that Moses, there was a very different one I want you to meet. A broken Moses. Before the power. Before the freedom. When you read these stories about Moses, which may be very familiar to you, I invite you to read with new eyes. Read this as a story of a broken, scared, confused man. Because when you do, I dare suggest that you will see a whole new story unfold – or maybe better said, a story within a story, as Moses walks through the rain, and much is revealed, both of who he really is, and who God really is.

Read Exodus 1:8-2:10

In verses 1:11-14, what was happening in Egypt just before Moses was born?

What are some of the words used to describe how the Israelites felt?

What was supposed to happen to Moses when/before he was born?

What did the midwives do in response to Pharoah's orders?

What was Pharoah's secondary order? If a son was born alive?

Stop for a minute and imagine the culture that Moses was born into. What are some of the feelings you think his mother might have felt while he was in utero?

Did you know that "during pregnancy, the parent's perception of the environment is chemically communicated to the fetus ... Though the developing child is "unaware" of the details (i.e., the stories) evoking the mother's emotional response, they are aware of the emotion's physiological consequences and sensations."

[https://birthpsychology.com. free-article/maternal-emotions-and-human-development]

So it's highly possible – even likely – that Moses was born with some emotional sensations from his mother's experience. **And while our past in no way defines us, it does sometimes help to explain us. Even to ourselves.**

There's also another side we glean about his mother and her strength. In Exodus 2:1-10, what is her response to Pharoah's second edict?

What does her response suggest to you about her personality and what Moses might have inherited from her?

What do you know about what was happening to your parents or in your culture when you were born?

Do you see any emotional patterns that you carry that may reflect those situations?

I carried a perpetual sense of doom with me for a long time. Just waiting for the other shoe to drop. God countered that one night with the word "Expectant." He wanted me to be expectant. I laughed. More of a bitter laugh than a hearty laugh. There I sat with an empty womb and a broken heart and He was telling me to be expectant? But it's because He was speaking against the lie that I felt doomed. Doomed to failure, doomed to loss. I was living a reactive life, hoping that I might prevent impending doom here and there. I later learned that when I was born, my father carried a huge fear of things going wrong. He didn't know Christ when I was born, and so he lived with a lot of fear. I'm not saying that I was pre-destined to this feeling of doom and fear, but I am saying that this world has hundreds of ways to expose us to fear and doubt, even in our earliest transformative moments. And so I carried it with me.

I wrote down "Expectant" in my journal on January 24, 2011, to counter-act the lie that I was doomed.

Are there any words or images that you perpetually fight against? **Ask God if He has a word or image for you to replace it with. When He gives it to you, write it here:**

Write what this word means to you:

Read Exodus 2:11-15

Moses experiences a lot in these four verses. The story jumps from his childhood to his adulthood abruptly, and his story continues with a very sudden turn of events. In these four verses Moses experiences a lot of emotions. Some are obvious, some we can infer from the story. All involve a level of sad, pain, hurt and loss.

Circle any of the feelings that you see (or can infer) from this passage:

Fear	Scared	Endangered	Selfish
Doubt	Happy	Unworthy	Strong
Anger	Vulnerable	Resentful	Confusion
Worry	Alone	Isolated	Grief
Anxiety	Control	Proud	Conflicted
Sadness	Desire	Misunderstood	Jealous
Frustration	Disappointment	Desperate	Fake
Confused	Denial	Hopeless	Exposed
Defenseless	Forgotten	Broken	Endangered

Now draw a box around any of the feelings that YOU can relate to or often feel.

It's really important, as we start this Study, to be honest about the things you're carrying. This is a space for just you and Jesus. It's sacred. Take some time and list some of the challenges YOU have faced or are facing, the sad you're carrying. Anything you are grieving the loss of.

Moses left a land of slavery but brought his pain with him. Pain can keep us captive just as much as chains can. But freedom – true freedom - is what He offers.

A prayer for today: your words to Him

God, I want to be brave and honest with my pain. I pray that you will protect me from being enslaved to it. I desire freedom. True freedom. Help me to dare to trust You with my hurts and wounds and confusion and fear. I know that my past does not define me. Help me to see myself as YOU see me, and above all, help ME see YOU in it.

A verse for today: His words to you

For you did not receive the spirit of slavery to fall back into fear, but you have received the Spirit of adoption as children, by whom you can cry "Abba! Father!"
– Romans 8:15

MOSES –
The thunder: Go Back to Egypt

Read Exodus 2:16-2:22

Where did Moses take his pain?

How is Moses described in verse 21?

Sometimes in the midst of pain, we experience reprieve. Moments where we feel "fine", or not much at all. I call these **Midian-moments**.

I experienced a Midian-moment after we had a failed adoption. It was a pain and a grief and a world of self-doubt that I'd never known before. I stepped back and decided to stop every attempt at parenting, be it infertility treatments or adoption applications, anything that required my brain to "go there".

> Midian can be an important place
> for us to stay for a bit, but we
> ## will always be foreigners there,
> and we shouldn't plan to stay.

Identify a Midian-moment in your life:

Do you think Moses was experiencing true contentment or "just fine"? What makes you think so?

Look at verse 22. How does Moses describe himself? What does this suggest to you?

Moses seems lost, right? In this passage we see his father-in-law making decisions for him; his wife making decisions for him; but very little of him taking initiative. Pain does this. It often leaves us reactive instead of proactive. From what you can see here, do you think Moses ever would have left Midian of his own initiative? Why or why not?

Read Exodus 3:1-4:31

God pursues Moses. **Don't miss that. He's the God who pursues.**
In 3:10, what does God ask Moses to do?

In 4:19, what does God offer Moses to show him that He understands what He's asking Moses to walk back into?

I will take you back to the place of your pain –
what must that have been like for Moses?
Not called somewhere new, but somewhere
painful, somewhere he had escaped.
And what does it mean for me?
I am fearful of what it could mean.
December 4, 2011

Does that mean that there was *no danger* to Moses?

Has God ever asked you to go back to a place of pain
(or is He asking you to now)?

Look at verses 3:11, 3:13, 4:1, 4:10, 4:13.
What are Moses' reasons for not wanting to go?

When God told me to go back to my place of pain, I gave a really spiritual answer. I said *"that's dumb."* Because it's like being asked to run into a burning building. And no one wants to do that. You only do it when there's *something worth rescuing inside.*

What are some of your reasons for not wanting to go back to a place of pain?

In verse 3:17, where does God say that this journey will take Moses? **Hint: It's not back to Midian.** That's important.

What does God say He will do in Egypt? See verses 3:20-22. How many times is the word "go" used in these verses?

Sometimes I wonder if Moses thought he would be going back to Midian.
God had something far greater in mind for him, as He does for us.

A prayer for today: your words to Him

God, help me to believe in the promise that You will answer. Help me to believe You are who you say You are and you do what You say you will do. And help me to understand the difference between what You say you will do and what I say you should do.

A verse for today: His words to you

Call to me and I will answer you, and will tell you great and hidden things that you have not known.

- Jeremiah 33:3

MOSES – Day 3
The storm gear: The Trust Dare

Read Exodus 5:1-9

Sometimes it gets worse before it gets better, doesn't it? Going into your pain hurts more sometimes than even when you were first there. If this is true for you, you are so not alone. **Moses had to dare to trust that God would show up.** *In* his doubts, *in* his fears, and *in* his confusion.

Who is Moses talking to in this conversation?

Pharoah was used to being the boss. Maybe we have traded Pharoahs for Presidents and Prime Ministers, and reduced some of their boss-like-qualities, but our hearts can still bow down to Pharoahs of fear, pain or hurt.

Have you ever heard any of your *Pharoahs* – your fears, pains or hurts - speak these lies to you?

❑ You are all alone.

❑ You are going nowhere.

❑ This is too much.

❑ This is all your fault.

❑ You deserve this.

❑ You are too much.

❑ This is going nowhere.

❑ No one cares.

❑ You are not enough.

Look at verse 2. What does Pharoah say?

You guys: our fears, our pains, our hurts - *__they don't know our God.__*

What is Pharoah trying to accomplish with the challenges he offers to Moses?

What are your fears, pains, and hurts trying to accomplish with their challenges?

Now look at verse 3. How does Moses respond? Who has he met with?

God wants to meet with you. Our *Pharoahs* - our fears, pains and hurts - will shout us down at every opportunity. **Stop** right now and tell YOUR Pharoahs about Who you're meeting with. Who your God is.

Read Exodus 5:15-23

I know, I KNOW. Moses just stood up to Pharoah. But remember, things were getting worse before they were getting better. So the people of Israel tracked him down and let him have it.

How many times have you stood up to your fears and pains and hurts, only to have another person's voice cause you to doubt? Maybe even someone you love? Maybe even someone who loves you? What was the hardest part about that?

Note what Moses does in verse 22. At first blush, we could see this as pure complaint from Moses. But I think there's something much deeper happening here. Because in this verse we see that Moses, having just stood up to Pharoah, is filled again with doubt and fear. So basically, he's normal. I love Moses for this because I may or may not relate. **But what he does with his doubt and fear is the powerful part. Who does Moses take his complaint to?**

How often do you take your complaint directly to God? I often complain *about* Him before I complain *to* Him.

If your doubts and fears are shouting in your ear, take them TO God directly, my friend. Seriously. Right now. Pray. And write out your prayer here:

Read Exodus 6:1-8

Who does God show Himself to be in response to Moses' complaint?

What does He promise Moses?

What can you take away from this passage as a promise to YOU today?

A prayer for today: your words to Him

God, I reject the lies of all the "Pharoahs" in my life. I want to be known as a person who has met with You. Who has spent time with Jesus. I want to see the difference that that makes in my life, and I want others to see it as well. Thank you for being a God I can bring my complaints to. Thank you for being a God that is the same yesterday, today and forever.

A verse for today: His words to you

Jesus Christ is the same yesterday, today, and forever.

- Hebrews 13:8

What God does here is seriously awesome. On a hundred levels. He shows His might and power and sovereignty. But that's not all. In these passages He is mightily strategic, mightily intentional, and mightily personal.

Read Exodus 2:9-10

Remember, Moses was raised in two homes. One that believed in the God of Israel. One that believed in a plethora of other gods, small g. I think it's fair to presume that Moses was really well educated about both, and equally fair to presume that he may have had a lot of confusion.

What Gods (big G or small g) were you raised to believe in?
This may include "none" or "self"

What gods (small g) are a part of your culture? Things that people work hard to please? For instance, you don't have to look far to say that my home culture of Orange County, CA worships the God of $$$.

Read Exodus 7:14-10:29

Power, storms, blood, frogs, gnats, hail … no wonder Charlton Heston signed up for this movie. This story has it all. But get this. With each plague, God wasn't just showing off. He was knocking down the gods of Egypt. Proving Himself to be the God of gods. The Lord of lords. The King of kings.

You could go crazy-deep with this stuff. I encourage you to. It's fascinating. But for our purposes check out the chart on the next page to get an idea of what was really going on as an epic battle-of-the-gods was being waged … and won

Plague	Egyptian god being defeated*
Water turned to blood	Khnum - Guardian of river's source. Hapi - Spirit of the Nile. Osiris - Nile was his bloodstream
Frogs	Hapi - Frog goddess to Egypt. Heqt - Related to fertility.
Gnats	Seb - The earth god of Egypt.
Flies	Uatchit - The fly god of Egypt. Yep, they had a fly god.
Livestock dies	Ptah, Mnevis, Hathor, Amon - Egyptian gods associated with bulls and cows.
Boils	Sekhmet - Egyptian goddess of Epidemics. Serapis – Egyptian god of healing. Imhotep – Egyptian god of healing.
Hail	Nut - Egyptian sky goddess. Isis & Seth - Egyptian agriculture deities. Shu - Egyptian god of the atmosphere.
Locusts	Serapia - Egyptian deity protector from Locusts.
Darkness	Ra, Amon-re, Aten, Atum, Horus – Egyptian sun gods. Thoth – Egyptian moon god.

*Source: http://www.biblecharts.org/oldtestament/thetenplagues.pdf

Unless we get hurt right out of every deception we have about ourselves, the word of God is not having its way with us.

– Oswald Chambers

I know, right? Ouch. One of my self-deceptions in pain is sometimes I don't feel "allowed" to, well, *feel*. I was in an avoidance pattern. And as God's Word was having its way with me, it hurt. Sometimes like hell. Yet it exposed the deceptions I held about myself, about others, and about my God.

Okay, our turn to knock down some little-g gods.

When we are led back to our place of pain, we need to do business with the little-g gods that live there.

Sometimes we don't even know there's a god we have in our life until the true God of gods is knocking it down.

In the chart on the next page, write in the left-hand column the "plagues" or "storms" that you can identify as you journey through your pain.

In the right-hand column, write the gods (small g) that you can identify as they get exposed and defeated.

This probably won't be filled out in one sitting – come back to it as many times as needed as you recognize the little-g gods who want to keep bossing you around.

Here is a sample chart from my journey through the grief of infertility.

Personal Plague/Storm	Personal god being exposed & defeated
Failed pregnancy test after failed pregnancy test	Control
No answers from doctors	Self-sufficiency, Knowledge
Disappointing husband, parents, self & friends	Pleasing others
Watching everyone else around me "get what they want when they wanted it"	Entitlement
Feeling like God was silent/cruel/absent/a jerk	A god who bowed to *my* whims and wishes (aka a god way too weak to worship)

Personal Plague/Storm	Personal god being exposed & defeated

Read Exodus 12:29-30

In this final plague, the God of Israel takes on the ultimate god of Egypt: Pharoah himself. The Egyptian people saw Pharoah as their god in the flesh. Pharoah saw himself as God in the flesh. Remember in Exodus 1, Pharoah commanded that all of Israel's sons be murdered before or just after their birth. Pharoah thought it was within his power, within his right, to determine who lived and who died. While this is a difficult passage if you focus on the death of Pharoah's child, it is a powerful passage when you focus on what God was doing in the big picture. Once and for all declaring Himself to be sovereign over everything, even life and death. And most especially over Egypt's final and most respected little-g god.

There was still one more god that had to be defeated in Moses' life: **the god of pleasing all the people**. *Gah, right?* I have that god too. And just like Moses, it's a lifetime lesson of knocking that god down. So take grace. God is the God of Gods, and He will continue to knock down all the other suckers pretending to be god. As many times as He has to.

A prayer for today: your words to Him

God, I want to give You permission to knock down the unworthy gods in my life. While I'm not a big fan of storms or plagues, I pray that you will give me eyes to see the things that need to be knocked over in my heart and in my life, so that I can see You and worship You as the only true and sovereign God of gods.

A verse for today: His words to you

And on that very day the Lord brought the people of Israel out of the land of Egypt.

– Exodus 12:51

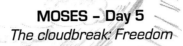

MOSES – Day 5
The cloudbreak: Freedom

Read Exodus 12:33-14:31

Freedom. Boom. I mean *come on*, did God deliver or did God deliver?

Write down what God says in verse 13:8

Write down what God says in verse 13:14, 16

This was not just about getting the Israelites out of Egypt. This was not just about getting Moses out of Egypt. This journey was about restoring *true freedom* to Moses and the people. This was about God establishing a whole new chapter in Moses' life. This was about God stamping a point in time that would forever change the lens through which Moses saw life.

Read Exodus 15:1-18

I don't know if Moses sang much before this, but if he did we certainly aren't given any earlier hints. I imagine it would be a lot like me saying "*and then I started dancing*" – it was probably rather shocking.

Key in on verse 11. How does Moses describe God?

Compare with Exodus 3:1-4:17.
What is different about how Moses is talking about God here in Exodus 15?

- 19 -

Knowledge informs us; experience transforms us.

Moses wasn't perfect when he came out of Egypt. He and God still wrestled. He still had doubts and fears here and there. But he also had a foundation. A marker in the road. A place to which he would never return. **He would never again be a slave to his pain.**

Look up the following passages:

Write down how Moses describes God in each of these passages:

Exodus 20:2:

Deuteronomy 1:30:

Deuteronomy 4:20:

Deuteronomy 6:12:

Deuteronomy 7:8:

When God calls us into our pain,
it's never because we are intended to stay there.

In order to find true freedom, Moses had to dare to go back to his place of pain. Remember, Moses was already *physically* out of Egypt back when he was in Midian. He didn't need to be physically rescued from Egypt – he had found his own solution to that. But he was still a captive to Egypt in many ways, never truly free from the wounds that haunted him until God took him back INTO his place of pain. Only then could he forever proclaim that God was the God who had taken him "out of Egypt."

Even today, Israel honors Moses and his leadership. He allowed God to work through his pain in such a way that it became a pillar not only for him, but for all of Israel.

A prayer for today: your words to Him

God, the prayer of my heart is for true freedom. The kind that only You can bring. And I pray that I would use my freedom to bring honor to Your name. To call attention to You. To know You for who You truly are, and to help others know that too.

A verse for today: His words to you

For freedom Christ has set us free; stand firm therefore, and do not submit again to a yoke of slavery.

– Galatians 5:1

WEEK 1 REFLECTION

Take time here to write down what you want to keep from this week. Go back through your notes and re-write things that stood out to you, what you had circled, notes that you underlined and nuggets you want to remember.

Pray for God to reveal one thing from this eek that He wants to cement deep in your heart about who He is and who you are. Remember that He who began a good work in you will be faithful to complete it.

Because God is _____

I know that I am _____

TWO ON THE ROAD – Day 1
The lightning strike: Loss, Death, Confusion, Lost Jesus

Meet the Two on the Road …

… This may be a familiar story to you. Two guys walking on the Road to Emmaus meet Jesus right after he rose from the dead. We don't really know much about them. Because that's not really the important part. But we do know they were followers of Jesus. And that part is important.

This story is commonly told at Easter. More proof that Jesus was in fact alive- alive after he died; he walked, talked, and ate with them. I've always read it as just that, just "more proof". In fact, in the Jewish culture of that day, the testimony of two witnesses was like solid gold. And in that respect, this is a story about the Resurrection of Christ, and more evidence, more proof that though He had died, He lives!

But it's not just about that. Something uh-maz-ing happens in this passage. Something I missed for the first three decades of knowing Jesus. Something intensely sacred – for them, and for us.

Read Luke 22:39-40, 47-62

Let's remember what these guys were carrying with them as they walked.

A disciple **betrays** Jesus.
A sword **fight** begins but is immediately ended.
Jesus is **arrested**.
Another disciple **denies** Jesus.
Jesus **dies.**

Betrays: deceives, reveals, gives up

Fight: struggle, dispute, attack

Arrested: seized, blocked, stopped

Denies: rejects, refuses, discards

**Just let these words sink in.
Because they were living them.**

Look at 22:39-40. What were they in the garden for right before this all took place?

I've been in that garden before. I don't mean the Garden of Gethsemane, although I've been there too and it should be on your bucket list because *Olive Trees.*

But I mean the garden where peace turns into chaos in a matter of minutes. Where things get really confusing and really scary and really hurtful. One of those gardens was our home Church. This was a place we loved. With people we loved. It was family. It was safe. Until it wasn't.

In a surprising (to me) turn of events, my husband, who worked there as a pastor, no longer had a job. And we no longer had a church home. The feelings of betrayal suffocated me. I was lost and disoriented and scared and HURT. But most of all I no longer felt safe.

Most of us have been in "that garden" - a time when you felt like you were in the right place doing the right thing but then something went terribly wrong.

Describe your garden of gethsemane. How did you feel?

What do you think Jesus' followers expected of Him that night?

Do you think that His followers expected He would ACTUALLY be arrested?

Look at 22:59. What does Jesus choose to act on?

Was it the ear of a follower or someone there as an enemy?

A defining moment for a child is when they realize their dad isn't superman after all ... and they have to decide whether to still love and trust him. Sometimes I treat God like Super-man, expecting Him to swoop in and save the day. AND HE IS IN THE BUSINESS OF SAVING. But sometimes even in the midst of saving our souls, the only thing we see being saved is a guy's ear.

Describe a time when you expected God to
swoop in and save the day
AND HE DID.

- 27 -

Describe a time when you expected God to
swoop in and save the day
AND IT FELT LIKE HE SAVED AN EAR INSTEAD.
Maybe even someone else's ear.
How did you feel?

How do you think Jesus' followers felt in the Garden that night?

Suffice it to say that this was a scary, confusing, chaotic night for Jesus'
followers. And let's remember that it wasn't just a confusing time to see what
was happening with Jesus. But also with each other. Amongst their very own.

When grief strikes, you turn to your people. Your tribe. The people that you
expect to have your back. But that night, Judas held the knife in
their backs. And Peter, well, he turned his back.

Describe a time that you've felt betrayed. Or been surprised by a friend's
behavior.

How did you react?

Read Luke 23:44-49

How does verse 46 describe Jesus' death?

Have you ever held on to hope until a "last breath"?

What changes when that last breath is taken?

Seven years ago, I sat at the bedside of our beloved Aunt Ruth as pancreatic cancer took her life.
We took turns sitting watch at her side. We knew what was coming. Her death was no longer a
question of if but when. I found myself praying "please let this be her last breath, please let this
be her last breath, please let this be her last breath" as the days progressed.
Anyone who's ever prayed that prayer knows how shocking it is to ask for such a thing.
You don't want it to be over. But you want it to be over.

When it really was THE end, I found myself changing my plea:
"just take one more breath, just take one more breath".

But when she breathed her last, I knew that hope of recovery was gone.
I hadn't even realized I'd help onto any hope of that. My head had long since crossed
the bridge of knowledge. Apparently my heart still had some fancy ideas that she
could still live. That there was still a chance for a miracle. I didn't really know I'd hoped
for that until her last breath took that hope away.

I can't help but wonder what miracles Jesus' followers were waiting for as they watched the night progress. What hopes were they holding onto? What hopes expired as he took his last breath? Jesus' death and resurrection was just about to change how we understand and respond to death for the rest of time. **But they didn't know that yet.**

As Jesus breathed his last, we see three very different responses.

Look at Luke 23:47.
How does the Centurion respond to Christ's last breath?

Look at Luke 23:48.
How do the crowds respond to Christ's last breath?

Look at Luke 23:49. How do Christ's followers respond to His last breath?

Why do you think that his followers stood at a distance?

**Sometimes standing at a distance
is as close as we can get to the
thing that is wrecking us.**

Have you ever "stood at a distance to watch" as something painful unfolds in your life?

Is there anything you're "standing at a distance" from right now?

And sometimes others – strangers even – have a clearer view of what's going on than we do. I mean, it wasn't the Centurion's best friend on the cross. The crowds of passersby didn't know the sound of Jesus' laugh over a campfire. His followers did. His followers were watching their best friend, their teacher, their Rabbi, their we-had-hoped-you-were-the-Messiah **die**.

They took some big questions with them on that
Road to Emmaus.

A prayer for today: your words to Him

God, am I standing at a distance from something that You're doing in my life? Something that I don't understand? Would you give me the courage to trust You in it? To edge a bit closer, where I can see more clearly?

A verse for today: His words to you

Salvation is nearer to you now than when you first believed.
– Romans 13:11

TWO ON THE ROAD – Day 2
The thunder: Be willing to learn

Read Luke 24:1-12

Look at verse 9. The two on the road were probably part of "all the rest" who heard the women's reports that Jesus was no longer in his tomb. Now look at verse 11. How did they respond to the reports the women brought back from the tomb? What did they think of them?

Is there any part of Jesus' story, Jesus' promises, that you have a hard time believing? Be honest. I mean, it's kind of a whacky story.

It's really hard to believe that things that are too good to be true are actually true.

Read Mark 9:14-27

This is one of my favorite stories of Jesus. Not just because of what happens with the boy, but because of what happens with the boy's father. Both are miracles.

Look at verse 18. What does the father say about why he's brought his son?

What does Jesus say is possible in verse 23?

Okay now here's my favorite part. Write down what the father says in verse 24:

Amen. Grace, grace. The boy's father had enough faith to bring his son to Jesus in the first place. He knew there was something that he couldn't do and he desperately hoped that this Jesus would be able to. And in that moment where Jesus is talking with him directly, he cries out *"YES! I do believe. But also, part of me doesn't. Help that part."* If there's any part of Jesus that you're having a hard time believing, make this the cry of your heart today. He will.

Read Luke 24:13-32

"That very day" two of them were going to Emmaus. What very day?

Who drew near? (Note: He is so the God who draws near. Just tuck that in your back pocket for later. And by "later" I mean every day of your life.)

And they don't recognize him. I know, it's weird. It's a mystery. Personally, I'm okay living with mysteries. Including this one. I don't do mystery-meat, but a mystery-God I can live with. It keeps Him interesting.

Also, I've not recognized Jesus in my life lots of times. You?

Look at verse 17. What do they do in response to Jesus' question?

Have you ever let yourself stand still and look sad? Sad is not a sin, you know. God draws near to broken hearts. In this fast-paced world, just standing still can feel like a sin. Add the looking sad part and most people just don't know what to do with you. Oh how I pray that we can know that with Jesus it's okay to stand still, looking sad when we need to.

Read Psalm 34:18

How is God described here?

Back to Luke 24. I love what they say next. *"Ummm, are you totally and completely clueless? Do you not know what's going on here?"* I may or may not have talked to Jesus that way before.

Look at verses 17 and 19 again. What questions does Jesus ask?

I think you could read these verses a few different ways.

> One is to presume that Jesus actually needed to be filled in.
> > *He didn't.*

> The other is to presume that Jesus was just looking for a way to fill time.
> > *He has endless supplies,*
> > *so I doubt that's it.*

> The other is to presume that Jesus *wanted* to be filled in.
> That he actually wanted them to voice what was going on
> inside their heads and hearts.
> > *Just so crazy that it's probably it.*

"Talk to me, tell me what's going on in that head and heart of yours."
- Jesus

Jesus also wants YOU to express yourself. Seriously. In the good and the bad and the hard and the messy. Sometimes we categorize "worship" as singing praise songs, expressing gratefulness, but here we see Jesus saying "talk to me, tell me what's going on", and in that is just as much worship as a happy song, my friend.

Worship, verb: to show worth

Look at Luke 24:19-24. List the things that they identify for Jesus as the goings-on in their heads and hearts and headlines ...

Now list some of YOUR goings-on ... show Him worth [worship] by simply telling Him what's in your head and heart today ...

Friday's Rain

A prayer for today: your words to Him

Thanks for being a God who doesn't need my help but does want my heart. Help me to remember that You are the God who draws near to me in my confusion, and that when I stand there looking sad you actually want to know all of my goings-on. Help me to show You worship by bringing my things to you.

A verse for today: His words to you

Cast all your cares on me, because I care for you.

– 1 Peter 5:7

TWO ON THE ROAD – Day 3
The storm gear: Listen

Read Luke 24:22-24

← We know this, we've seen this, we heard this …
what we don't know is WHERE IS JESUS? →

This is the first question when loss strikes, right?

Some cry it in sincerity … *Where are you right now, God?*

Some scream it in anger … *Where the @!%[! are you!?!?!?*

Some whisper it in quiet desperation … *God, are you there?*

Some offer it as a taunt … *SO, where's your God NOW!?*

No matter how it crosses our lips, the question we ask is the same that the two on the road asked that day.

We know this is happening here. We've seen that over there. We've heard rumors. *But we have no idea where Jesus is right now.*

Identify a time in your life where you wondered where Jesus was.

Jesus could have gone for a "ta-da!" moment. Honestly, I'm kind of surprised He didn't. And honestly, a lot of times when I'm looking for Him I want the "ta-da!" But He offers them something even more amazing. He shows them how to see Him whether or not He's standing right there.

The answer they receive is also the same answer for us today. But it's quite different than a lot of the "answers" we often offer each other today.

Have you ever noticed that people – and, I hate to say it, but, mostly Christians – try to offer quick solutions to pain?

We are uncomfortable with no answers.

We are uncomfortable with slow answers.

We are uncomfortable with being uncomfortable.

Circle any of the "quick fixes" you've heard offered in response to pain – maybe yours, maybe someone else's:

God must have a better plan.

Everything happens for a reason.

You just need to have faith.

Well, His ways are mysterious.

I guess I just have an extra dose of faith.

Maybe I just have more grace than some people; _____ never really bothered me.

When He closes a door, He opens a window.

Have you prayed about it?

But they're in a better place now!

God works all things together for good.

God won't give you more than you can handle.

If you have ever wanted to punch someone in the face after hearing one of these statements, draw a box around it.

Offering a spiritual cliché to comfort someone is like dumping snow down their pants expecting them to get warm.
– Jedd Medefind
President, CAFO

See, the thing is, there is truth in these statements. But when offered alone, they are incomplete truths. **And when we offer incomplete truth, it produces incomplete results.** We miss the chance to see not just where Jesus is, but more about WHO He is.

Here's what I mean. Jesus could have gone for the "ta-da!" moment, He could have just instantly revealed Himself. He was right there. **But this piece of the truth would have only answered a part of their hurt and doubts.** They would have missed WHO He was because they were focused on WHERE He was.

And all too often, we toss a "ta-da!" at each other in moments of pain or confusion. Jesus offers another way.

Read Luke 24:27

What does Jesus do?

Jesus cared more about them understanding the bigger picture, the deeper meaning, the wilder-than-their-imagination answer than He did about a quick fix.

When your punch-o-meter goes off the next time that someone hands you a spiritual cliché, it's time to head to God's Word like Jesus did on that Road.

Step 1. Identify the questions that your emotions reveal.

"Emotions reveal questions, not answers."
– Jason Miller

Jason's my husband. He's smart. He's taught me that we have to let our emotions lead us to identify the questions our heart is wrestling with, because we can't find a clear answer without a clear question.

Another smart guy did this well. His name is David. Best known for killing Goliath and authoring most of the Psalms.

Read Psalm 77:1-6

David lets his emotions reveal his questions.
Write out the emotions he identifies in verses 1-4.

In verses 5-6, he describes what he is doing. Note the end of verse 6 – how does David describe what his spirit is doing?

David sets a brave example for us. He dared to speak plainly and openly. He dared to say things like "*you know what, God, I'm not really sure that you are good right now.*" His emotions revealed the question of whether God was good, but for the *answer*, he went on a diligent search. **Don't let yourself stop at the question and treat it like the answer.**

Write the questions that David asked about God in verses 7-9. Note that part of our diligence is daring to be this honest.

Just about every emotion has this at the core:
>   *Is God ACTUALLY good? Can I ACTUALLY trust Him?*

Pick a spiritual cliché that bugs you. Use the list on page 38 if one doesn't immediately come to mind.

Then complete these sentences. Identify your feelings, your emotions.

Hearing this platitude makes me feel like I am ...

Hearing this platitude makes me feel like God is ...

Now turn those feelings into questions. Remember, the emotion, the feeling, reveals questions, not answers.

So I wonder if I am ...

And I wonder if God is ...

Note: This often takes time. It may not happen just through an exercise. But pay attention, as you go through your days ahead, to what you're seeing and questioning about yourself. And about God. And write down the questions you see as you see them.

Step 2. Go where answers actually exist.

There are so many good apps out there. When I'm in a new city, I love looking up reviews on restaurants and things to do. I want to know what others have found. This is good and fun and wonderful, but I don't actually KNOW what that burger tastes like just by reading a review. I have to go throw down some cash and take a bite myself. The same is true in looking for answers about who we are and who God is. While books and stories from others can be good hints, good reviews, nothing replaces getting in and tasting it for yourself. Don't ever let anything replace God's Word as your source of truth.

Read Psalm 77:10-12

What does David say he will do?

Read Acts 17:10-11

How are these Jews described? What did they do with the Scriptures?

Read 2 Timothy 3:16

How is Scripture described? What is it good for? "Profitable for"?

Read Hebrews 4:12

List the four different ways God's word is described here:

Ask God to truly speak through His Word and guide you personally as you head into step 3.

- 42 -

Step 3. Hunt and gather.

Brainstorm words that are related to the questions you've identified in Step 1. Use a thesaurus (look at both synonyms and antonyms) or a dictionary or an app. Or a pencil. Those are actually shockingly effective. Doodling can lead to some amazing discoveries. Write some of the words here.

Take your list of words and start looking for Scripture verses that talk about these things. Use a concordance or the back index of your Bible.
Write some you find here.

Read through these references. Write down the ones that stand out to you. Write them out in their fullness. Use more space as necessary. We retain more this way. We see more this way. And we want to see more.

Step 4. Taste and see.

Read Psalm 77:13-20

I wonder if David took a big pause between verses 12 and 13. Where he actually spent time just pondering and remembering. This is his "I know that God is … " list:

Psalm 77:13

Psalm 77:14

Psalm 77:15

Psalm 77:16

Psalm 77:17

Psalm 77:18

Psalm 77:19

Psalm 77:20

While at first glance these declarations don't speak to the questions he raised in verses 7-9, **David actually offers answers that are bigger and deeper than the questions He posed.** Just like our friends heading to Emmaus, His questions started with WHERE ARE YOU. The answers landed on WHO ARE YOU. That's often how it works.

Ok, now you take a bite. A big, deep bite of the truth you've just found. Using the verses you've just written down in step 3, complete these sentences. Add space as necessary.

I know that God is ...

I know that I am ...

A prayer for today: your words to Him

God, you are a mystery. I don't always know where You are. I can't always see You in my life, even when You're right there with me. But I'm so glad that You are a God who doesn't leave me with a quick fix because you care more about my deeper healing and understanding than you do about ending the awkwardness or the hurt of the moment. Help me replace platitudes with power. And help me to be a person who sees WHO you are even when I can't see WHERE you are.

A verse for today: His words to you

I am with you always, even to the end of the age.
— Matthew 28:20b

← Beginning with Moses and all the prophets, He interpreted to them in all the Scriptures the things concerning himself. →

Read Luke 24:27

So Jesus does not give the "ta-da!" in verse 25.

Instead he offers them something deeper, something more powerful. *"I need to show you something that's even more amazing than the fact that I'm alive right now. I am going to show you how you can find me even when I'm not walking alongside you."*

This is for us, my friends. If Jesus had done a nice "ta-da!" for these two, the story would be a nice one to keep tucked away for Easter. But this story is for our everyday. **Because it is a blueprint to find Jesus.**

Is Jesus always with us? YES.

Can we always see it? NO.

How do we find Him? IN HIS WORD.

Today we are going to spend time with Moses and the prophets. Pure Bible-Study-Style. While this is by no means an exhaustive study of what Moses and the prophets said about Jesus, it is worth our while to take this path through Scripture IN ORDER TO SEE JESUS. My hope for today is simple: that we will respond with what I imagine the two on the Road to Emmaus said ... *"Oh. Wow."*

Beginning with Moses ...

I just love that we begin with Moses. Beginning with the guy who was brought through his pain. The guy who would have stayed in Midian if he'd had his way about it.

I wish we knew exactly what verses Jesus used here. We don't. But we can get some clues from other passages and quotes that his disciples referenced.

Read John 1:45

How is Jesus described?

Read Acts 3:22-23

Write down what Peter quotes Moses as saying:

Compare with Deuteronomy 18:15-22

Cool, huh?

There are a few different opinions about what Moses meant by "a prophet like me." It's worth a deeper study, but for our purposes I believe at its base the "like me" part is that Moses was the *original* intermediary between God and man. Jesus is the *final* intermediary between God and man.

Read 1 John 2:1

How is Jesus described?

What does He do on our behalf?

Read Numbers 21:4-9

Why did Moses lift up a serpent in the wilderness?

What was the result if someone looked at the serpent?

Read John 3:14-15

Who does Jesus say has to be lifted up like that serpent?
Note: the 'Son of Man' is a reference to Jesus the Christ, the Messiah.

For what purpose? What result?

Read Psalm 22:1-18

Draw a line between the verses that match up what the Psalmist wrote thousands of years before Jesus' life, and the way in which Jesus died.

Psalm 22:15   Matt. 27:46

Psalm 22:18   Matt. 27:34

Psalm 22:7-8   Matt. 27:39-44

Psalm 22:1   Matt. 27:35

Read Isaiah 52:13-53:12

Each of these parallel passages, written thousands of years apart, tell a compelling story of Christ and his suffering. For each pairing below, write the type of suffering described.

Isaiah 53:5 & 1 Peter 2:24:

Isaiah 53:7 & Matthew 26:57-64:

Isaiah 52:14 & Mark 15:16-20:

Read Luke 16:19-31

If someone refuses to hear what Moses and the Prophets say, what else will fail to convince them?

I find this story about Lazarus and the Rich Man particularly compelling when you think about the fact that AS THE RISEN CHRIST walking on the Road to Emmaus, Jesus *still* took them back to Moses and the Prophets for proof of Who He is.

Read 1 Peter 3:18

Why did Christ suffer?

Read John 3:16-17

Why did God send Jesus into the world?

A prayer for today: your words to Him

Oh. Wow.

A verse for today: His words to you

Yeah, I loved the world that much. I love you that much.

                               – John 3:16

TWO ON THE ROAD – Day 5
The cloudbreak: He is here

"As we befriend our pain – or, in the words of Jesus, "take up our cross" – we discover that the resurrection is, indeed, close at hand."

– Henri Nouwen

Read Luke 24:31-35

They met with Jesus.

He befriended their pain.

He laid out the Scriptures.

They now had a new Story.

What do you think it means to "befriend our pain"?

How was that modeled by Jesus and the two on the road?

Have you ever had a time where "your eyes were opened, and you recognized Jesus"? A time when you didn't think He was very involved in your life except when you look backwards? If so, describe.

← THEY REALIZED HE HAD BEEN WITH THEM THE WHOLE TIME. →

In verse 32, how do they describe how they felt while with Jesus?

Are you experiencing Jesus in the Scriptures? Are you letting Him interpret all the things concerning Himself? Are you letting Him show you where He is?

He doesn't always offer answers.
HE ALWAYS OFFERS HIS PRESENCE.

This is the power of this story, you guys. Of our stories. Of our pain. Jesus did not ignore their pain, and He also didn't "fix" it. He showed them where He was in it. Jesus doesn't ignore or fix our pain. But He always shows us where He is in it.

What do they do in verses 33-35?

What did they tell those gathered?

That's what we do with a good story. We re-tell it. It's why good stories spread like wildfire on Social Media: we like sharing.

If Jesus had gone for the "ta-da!", they would have had a cool story to tell – they would have said "HEY GUYS, JESUS WAS RIGHT THERE!" But instead, Jesus gave them a much bigger story to tell. I imagine the scene in Jerusalem to be something like this, with an open set of scrolls sprawled out and a lot of excited pointing:

"You guys, He's here …
and here …
and here …

and here ...
and here ...
and HERE!"

Jesus had just revealed Himself in such a way that **the Story just got bigger. Much. Bigger.**

It's the story we are still telling today. He is here. And here. And here. And here.

Are you willing for your Story to get bigger?
Write out a prayer in your own words about that:

Write down how God is described in each of these passages:

Deuteronomy 31:8:

Joshua 1:9:

Isaiah 41:10:

Isaiah 43:1-7:

Isaiah 65:24:

Matthew 28:20b:

I am here. And here. And here. And here.
– God.

- 53 -

Read John 20:30-31

Why are these things written down?

Read John 21:25

Wouldn't you love to know all about the other things that Jesus did? It's like an unfair movie trailer, right? Someday we'll know. What does John say about how many books it would take?

How many books would it take to write about what Jesus is doing in your life? Some of you may say "it wouldn't be a book, it would be a post-it note." Ok. Then write the post-it note. Because it's actually part of a much bigger Story. One which all the books in the world could not contain.

A prayer for today: your words to Him

You are the God who is here. And here. And here. Help me to see You as the God who walks beside me even when I can't see You. Help me to see You as the God who is telling a big big story. And help me to tell that Story well, as someone's who's heart burns within me.

A verse for today: His words to you

You will seek me and find me. When you seek me with all your heart, I will be found by you.

– Jeremiah 29:13-14a

WEEK 2 REFLECTION

Take time here to write down what you want to keep from this week. Go back through your notes and re-write things that stood out to you, what you had circled, notes that you underlined and nuggets you want to remember.

Pray for God to reveal one thing from this eek that He wants to cement deep in your heart about who He is and who you are. Remember that He who began a good work in you will be faithful to complete it.

Because God is _____

I know that I am _____

PETER – Day 1
The lightning strike: Denial, Identity Crisis, Friday

Meet Peter …

… The guy who walked on water. The first disciple recruited. The fisherman turned fisher-of-men. The preacher at the first mega-Church.

But also the guy who denied Jesus. Not once, not twice, but three times.

Talk about grief. Talk about getting real. I wonder how many times between Christ's arrest and ascension Peter wondered who he was. Really. Was he the guy who walked on water or walked away? Yes. And also, was he Simon or Peter or Simon-Peter. Yes, yes and yes. But more than all of that, he's the guy who was loved. So so loved.

Note: W./E. would be an amazing soundtrack to listen to while you do this Study; it was amazing to write it to. Just sayin'. You're welcome.

Read Matthew 4:18-20

Who was the first disciple Jesus called?

What was Jesus' promise to Peter?

When did Peter decide to follow Jesus?

There are very few things I've done "immediately" in my life; you?

Stop now and pray for this kind of courage. The kind of boldness that will **immediately** follow Jesus when He calls you into something.

GAH! I know, it's a hard prayer!

Friday's Rain   © Brooke Mardell, 2016, v.2

It was late. Dark. And we couldn't find anyone who could speak English. I was so so scared. Jason's fever was climbing. His aches increasing. He had had two bouts of Malaria before – this was different. Worse. I was afraid that it was what I was afraid of. Dengue Fever. All night I worked on his cramped muscles, took his temperature, and prayed. Like I've never prayed before – literally. Dengue Fever is not as dangerous as Malaria in that it's not guaranteed to kill you if left untreated, but ... there's no treatment. So it's actually more scary. In leaving home for Asia, it was the one disease that sent me into the fetal position in my heart. And now I was pretty sure he had it.

By daybreak, we were able to find out about an Australian Dr. who was about 45 minutes away. We packed up, got in a taxi, and I went through the thermometer routine. Normal. I checked again. Normal. *Wait, what?* And the cramps. Gone. Like someone had flipped a light switch off. By the time we got to the doctor, Jason felt like his normal self.

But we're no dummies - we know that diseases can play tricks, so in we went for tests. The Dr. poked and prodded and drew blood and sat down with a quizzical look on his face. *"Everything you've described is consistent with Dengue,"* he said. *"But I can't explain his sudden drop in fever. That's just not how Dengue works."* I knew in that moment that I could either choose to shrug my shoulders and say "huh, weird" or raise my hands and say "amen! Allelujah!". I've never since doubted that God chose to miraculously heal my husband that day in that taxi. I don't need a picture of that moment in order to see it instantly in my mind's eye. Since then, he's had other medical tricks and traumas, and we both go back to that day because we KNOW that if God chooses to, He can flip a switch and bring instant healing, defying doctors opinions. We also know He doesn't always choose to.

I had known "God can heal" my whole life, but then He came into MY home, so to speak, and healed MY husband, and I KNEW KNEW it.

More than a Disciple: a Friend

Read Mark 1:35-37

Where had Jesus gone and why?

Who went looking for him?

This might be one of my favorite verses about Jesus and Peter. I just love the simplicity, as I think about a dark early morning, quiet and hushed, and a heart that wakes up and thinks "I must find Him". And then he does.

Read Mark 1:29-31

Where did Jesus go? What does Jesus do there?

It's one thing to hear about miracles being done around the world. Or even around your neighborhood. But when it's in your OWN HOME, with YOUR family (and let's be real, with your **mother-in-law**), that's a whole new level of intimacy. Describe a time Jesus was "in your home", in YOUR family. Maybe He didn't heal anyone of a miraculous fever, but you KNEW He was there. Present. Active. Real. How did that affect or change your relationship with Jesus?

Note: If there's no time that you can recall Jesus being "in your home", invite him there now.
Check out Revelation 3:20; someone's at the door.

- 59 -

Read Luke 8:51-55

Who is allowed into the room with Jesus? What were they allowed to see?

Read Luke 9:28-35

Who were the three invited to witness the Transfiguration?

In these passages, we get these small glimpses of Jesus having a *friendship* with some of His disciples. Maybe even some besties. He had friends, not just followers. In a world rather addicted to "followers", make sure you have friends too.

Read Matthew 26:36-41

Jesus is in the garden. Just before his betrayal and arrest.
Who does he invite to go with him?

In verse 37, what does He allow them to see that no one else does?

In verse 38, what does He ask of them?

In verse 41, who does Jesus direct His question to?

Who are your "safe people"?

There are unsafe people. And there are safe people who make mistakes. In the midst of pain it can get real tricky to know the difference. Seek good counsel and ask the Lord for wisdom to now who's who. Jesus doesn't base his "safe people list" on a perfect track record. Peter was a one-of-us-kind-of-guy, full of doubts and questions and putting his foot in his mouth all the time. So don't base your "safe people list" on perfection.

More than Denial: a Freefall

Fill in this timeline of events by writing what Peter says or does in each verse/section:

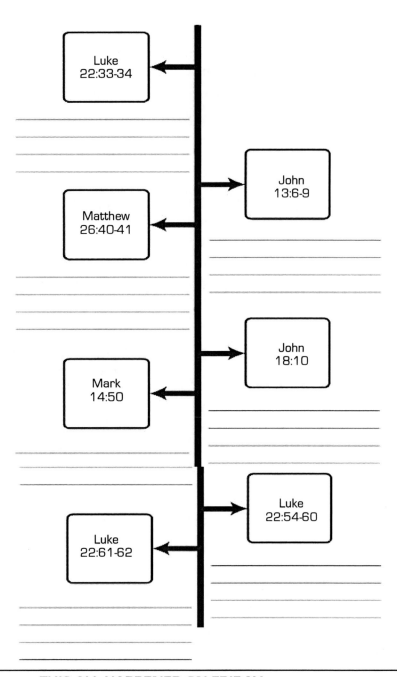

Have you ever spiraled? Describe a time when you went from a height of faith to a valley of doubt in a short amount of time.

Are you ever tempted to give yourself score cards in those moments? And define yourself by the "average point score"? Remember that Jesus sees the whole person – wholly bold, wholly broken. And we don't see him keeping score. So neither should we.

Read John 13:36-38

Peter was actually right. But so was Jesus. Peter did later die for the sake of Christ. He followed Him all the way to death. He also denied Him first. And then a second time. And then a third time.

I've never had so much food in my life as when we were in Bangladesh. Seriously, the most generous people ever. Every time we were invited for "tea", it was a full meal. And I would say "no, thank you" and they would heap a pile of delicious food on my plate anyways. *Gah*, I thought, *no does not mean no here.*

I (eventually) learned that my first no didn't mean no. Nor did my second. One or two "no's" is just a polite way of saying "yes please". **Only a third "no" was heard as a "no, for real."**

This is a lot like the culture of Peter's time; three times of repetition signaled a sense of finality, completion.

Have you ever felt like you failed at something significant? If so, what? Describe.

Have you ever felt disqualified from serving Jesus? If so, why? Describe.

Read 1 Cor. 1:27

Fill in the blanks.

But God chose what is _____ to shame the wise;

God chose what is _____ to shame the strong.

So BOOM. And amen.

If you've ever felt disqualified from ministry, then you're in good company. So did the first Pastor.

A prayer for today: your words to Him

Come into my home, my family. I welcome you as a friend. I'd love to be besties. And I'm so glad you don't keep score. You don't see me for my average. I sometimes go high and low IN THE SAME DAY. But you choose to use foolish and weak things to shame the wise and strong things, so have at. Here I am.

A verse for today: His words to you

Behold, I stand at the door and knock. If anyone hears my voice and opens the door, I will come in to him and eat with him and he with me. – Revelation 3:20

PETER – Day 2
The thunder: Do you love me?

So *that* Friday. Fill this in from **Luke 22:62.**

Peter wept _____.

I so get Peter. I so totally and completely get Peter. That Friday was filled with broken hearts, broken hopes, broken dreams, broken expectations, broken plans. So yeah, he wept. Bitterly.

Each of us has our Fridays.
Those days, weeks, months, or years of broken pieces.

What's your Friday?
What are some of the broken pieces you're carrying?
Broken heart? Broken dream? Broken plan?

> "If through a broken heart God can bring His purposes to pass in the world, then thank Him for breaking your heart."
> – Oswald Chambers
>
> This makes me want to break Oswald's face.
> *November 1, 2011*

I cried so many tears on my Friday. I, like Peter, learned things I didn't want to know. **About my Hero. About myself.** Friday was dark, and painful, and ugly, and terrifying, and opened places of his own soul that Peter wishes he'd never seen. And certainly wishes no one else had seen.

Here's the thing about Friday. On Friday, Peter saw things about himself and his God that he didn't want to be true. That he couldn't believe were true.

What did you see about yourself that you didn't want to be true on your Friday?

What did you see about your God that you didn't want to be true on your Friday?

Friday was about much more than whether or not Peter was trying to save his own skin. Jesus knew that. Peter knew that. Let's dig a bit deeper into Peter here to see what was at stake.

Read John 1:35-42

Who was Simon/Peter's brother?

Who was Andrew a disciple of before he followed Jesus?

What was he seeking?

So Peter was invested. With a brother who was a disciple of John the Baptist, he had already put a lot of time and heart into this search. On the night he denied Christ, he was denying a lot more than three years of his life.

Read Matthew 15:10-20

In verse 15, who is asking for this to be explained?

Look at verse 18. What comes out of the mouth proceeds from the_____

Peter wanted to understand this. He asked the question. I can't help but wonder if Peter carried the weight of these words with him as he recognized that his WORDS of denial proceeded from a HEART of doubt and fear.

Have you ever been surprised by something that comes out of your mouth?

Have you ever stopped to see what that says about what's in your heart? I'm not talking about the four-letter bomb that flies out of your mouth when you stub your $@!% toe. I mean, there are reasons that cuss words were invented, after all. I'm talking about the subtler things that cross our lips from time to time. The things we snidely say about this friend, or that place, or subjects we find ourselves bringing up over and over again.

Stop now. Think. Be honest. What are some items you "regularly" hear come across your lips that surprise you?

Take a few guesses about what it may say about what's in your heart.

This heart → mouth correlation can also be a place of power.
Of salvation.

Read Romans 10:9-10

How does one get saved, according to verse 9?

What is the correlation between the heart and the mouth in verse 10?
Which comes first?

_____ -> _____

So our friend Peter, he did some foolish things but he was no fool. He knew that this denial crossing his lips three times in a row revealed something in his heart – something he probably didn't even know was there before.

I may or may not have what some would call a "control issue". And so we had "that fight" again. The one we've had a hundred times. I say this, he says that. Except this time he said something different. And it stopped me in my tracks. *"How many times are you going to ask me that before you trust me?"* he said. *"This has nothing to do with not trusting you"* I retorted. *"Yes, it does. Because your questions tell me that your heart still doubts me. So I'll keep answering these questions until that doubt dies."* You guys, he was so right. And I so hated it. Not only the him-being-right part, but what he was right about.

What was crossing my lips was revealing what was inside my heart. It's tricky business, but sometimes we have to pay attention to those cues, because sometimes we need to see what's inside our heart, even if we don't like it. It's the only way we can kill it.

- 67 -

Read Luke 12:8-9

What does Jesus say will happen if someone denies him before men?

Let's assume (I think safely so) that Peter remembered these words, too. Describe in your own words how you think Peter would have felt that Friday night.

Spoiler alert: This wasn't the end of the story.

Read John 6:66-69

What does Jesus ask in verse 67?

What is Peter's response?

Friday wasn't Peter's only chance to get away. Nor was it the only time he considered that following Jesus could be dangerous.

> "To what will you look for help if you
> will not look to that which is
> stronger than yourself?"
> — C.S. Lewis, *Mere Christianity*

Read Luke 22:61

What does Jesus do in this verse?

The look. GAH!

Right between the look and the weeping, what does Peter do?

I think he remembered a whole lot more than "oh yeah, Jesus said I would deny Him." I think he remembered all that we've just read. And more.

See here's the thing. It would be one story if we were just looking at a guy who got confused in a garden one night, got scared and shied away from knowing the friend who was heading towards crucifixion. But there's a much bigger story that unfolded on that fateful Friday. **A much bigger piece of Peter got lost that night as those words of denial crossed his lips.** A nail was about to pierce Jesus' skin, and a sword had just sliced through Peter's soul.

Is there a part of your soul that has been sliced by Friday?

A Prayer for Today: your words to Him

God, sometimes I wish I was still oblivious. I wish that I didn't know what _____ felt like. I wish I didn't know how painful the sword's cut could be. I wish I didn't know the battle love had to fight. But I'm so glad that's not where the story ends. That something comes after the sword. Help me to watch for your GRACE today.

A verse for today: His words to you

The people who survive the sword will find grace in the wilderness.
–   Jeremiah 31:2

Write the word "GRACE" somewhere that you will see it today. On your hand, on the lock screen of your phone, on twitter, on a post-it note on your desk. Wherever your eyes are going to find it.

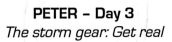

PETER – Day 3
The storm gear: Get real

Read John 13:1-11

> "He will do with you what He
> is not doing with other people."
> – Oswald Chambers

What is Peter's first response to Jesus' offer?

What is Peter's second response to Jesus' offer,
after the "terms" are clarified?

Peter's identity was that of a disciple. It's a label he wore for three years+.

Identity matters. When looking for our identity, there are a lot of places to look: our culture, our friends, ourselves and our own expectations. The thing is, those are constantly in flux, constantly subject to change, so we feel constantly instable, insecure, and incomplete.

We live in a society of labels. Some may be things you love and are proud of, others not so much.

Here's some of my "labels", for better and for worse:

- Attorney
- Infertile
- Wife
- Traveler
- Furmom (yes, that's a thing)

- Daughter
- Christian
- American
- Sister
- Friend

Friday's Rain

Your turn. What are some of your "labels"? Include the ones you love, and the ones you don't so much.

The thing about labels is that they can't capture who we really are. But we can become quite attached to them. So can others.

Some of the "labels" we see attached to Peter are

Fisherman
Disciple
Follower
Galilean
Friend

That Friday, Peter lost some of his major labels in one fell blow.

Look closer at **Mark 14:66-71**

Aren't you a **follower** *of Jesus?* → No

Yes, you're a **disciple***.* → No.

You are a **Galilean** *though.* → No.

Identity crisis much? As painful as Friday can be, sometimes we need our labels taken away in order to find out who we really are.

Read Philippians 3:4-11

Here Paul tackles his identity – all the things he's proud of. List the things Paul lists as part of his identity, some of his "labels":

Compared to knowing Christ, what does Paul call this list?

> Surrender is a tough thing.
> Unless you think about how many things
> you surrender to your garbage can each week.
> - Robyn Paynter

Go to Acts 26

What expectations ruled Paul's life before he met Jesus? (verses 4-12)

What changed when he met Jesus? (13-18)

Can you see labels and expectations and emotions that ruled who you were before you met Jesus?

Circle any that still do.

Pray to release those. I know, I KNOW! All the tough prayers.

"Give me all of you!!! I don't want so much of your time, so much of your talents and money, and so much of your work. I want YOU!!! ALL OF YOU!! I have not come to torment or frustrate the natural man or woman, but to KILL IT! No half measures will do. I don't want to only prune a branch here and a branch there; rather I want the whole tree out! Hand it over to me, the whole outfit, all of your desires, all of your wants and wishes and dreams. Turn them ALL over to me, give yourself to me and I will make of you a new self—in my image. Give me yourself and in exchange I will give you Myself. My will, shall become your will. My heart, shall become your heart."
— C.S. Lewis, *Mere Christianity*

A prayer for today: your words to Him

ALL of me!? Gah, ok, but I also want all of You.

A verse for today: His words to you

Abide in me, and I will abide in you.

– John 15:4

You guys ... I'm so over-the-moon with what Jesus does here that I can't even.

Because what He did with Peter, He does with us.

Read Luke 24:1-12

What does Peter do when he hears the women's news?

Where did he go next?

And doing/feeling what?

Marvel, verb: to become filled with surprise, wonder, or amazed curiosity

I have sat in a sacred waiting room much like the Upper Room where the disciples waited.
Trying to wrap my head and heart around watching my best friend dying.
Preparing for a funeral. I mean, you guys, the women went to the
tomb *to prepare the body for burial,* not to check for resurrection.

And the women came and Peter probably stood. Or maybe he only half looked up.
Because either way, he already knew what they were there to say.

They came to pronounce that they had prepared the body.
I, too, stood to receive the pronouncement
when the doctors walked in the waiting room.
But you guys: **"He is alive!" is news that makes you RUN.**

Read John 21:1-14

I love Peter here.

I've always heard it said that Peter went back to fishing as a sign of defeat. I'm not so sure. I mean, Peter's really the only one who can tell us someday. But Luke 24:12 says he was marveling. My best guess is that this fisherman just didn't think the story was continuing. He didn't know what to make of it. And he sure as heck didn't think he had any further part to play. Me thinks his best thinking was probably done over a fishing net. And he had a lot of thinking (marveling) to do.

And oh how I love Jesus here. Because He came and found Peter. **He finds us, you guys.**

What does Peter do when he realizes it is Jesus at the seashore?

Read Luke 5:1-11

What mirrored details exist in both times that Jesus calls to Peter?

What is different about how Peter responds here versus in John 21:1-14?

That Peter. He knows how to fall out of a boat.
I want to do more boat-falling in my life.

Read John 21:15-19

I've always read this story as a bit of a reprimand, to be honest. Peter denied Christ three times, now he has to affirm him three times. But I was wrong. So wrong.

Because with these three questions, Jesus isn't "correcting" Peter – He's restoring Him.

Jesus isn't interested in correcting you; He's interested in restoring you. Sometimes that requires correction, but that's never the end, only the means.

With these three questions, Jesus isn't ignoring what happened – in fact, He's saying "*Peter, we gotta go into this. Together.*" It's one of the most intense DTR (Define-the-Relationship) talks of the Bible.

A little Greek detour is necessary here. Because what we translate as "love" has a few different meanings.

> **Agape** love = intense, complete, devoted sacrificial love, even if you do not like him or her
>
> **Phileo** love = brotherly affection, friendship

In the first two questions, Jesus asks Peter, "Do you AGAPE me?"

And Peter answers "I PHILEO you."

So basically, Jesus is saying "*Peter, do you love me even if you still don't like me right now?*" And Peter's answer is more along the lines of "*Jesus I really like you – it's actually the love part that I'm still not so sure about.*" This kind of honest answer could only come from one who has searched his heart. While he wept. While he fished. While he ran to the tomb. While he marveled.

> "It was an honest assessment of where [Peter] was.
> **Don't ever boast of how much you love Jesus;**
> **boast of how much Jesus loves you.**
> Our love is fickle. It runs hot and cold.
> But God's love for us never changes.
> It is always there."
> – Greg Laurie

Read Psalm 139

Pay special attention to verses 23-24.
What does David invite God to do here?

Look at verse 19; David didn't exactly write this in a peaceful state of mind. What does he want God to do in this verse?

This invitation – search me and know my heart – is dangerous. Know my anxious thoughts. See if there be any wrong way in me. That's a much more difficult prayer than it sounds like. **It means opening up the deep places, the dark places, and saying "let's explore" – and to explore means, inherently, that you don't always know what you'll find.** Or like it once it's found. But to keep the walls up against exploring is to keep mysteries hidden even from ourselves.

Look at verse 24. Where does David want this search to lead?

Search me, know me, show me, lead me.
- David

Is there a part of your heart that needs to be restored? Pray through this prayer of David's and write down what God shows you …

Search me. Ok God, I give you permission to search me. I open up these anxious thoughts to you:

Know me. Are there any grievous ways in me?

Show me. What parts do You need to restore?

Lead me. What's your path through this?

Back to John 21:15-21

Jesus' third question turns an interesting corner. He doesn't ask Peter a third time about AGAPE love. I think there's an interesting hint to Peter – and to us – here. Remember, repeating something three times led to a sense of finality, completion. And Jesus knew this was not yet final – Peter wasn't done marveling. He didn't "close the door" on AGAPE love returning to Peter's heart. But He does meet Peter where he's at, as if to say **"So, you like me. Ok, let's start there."**

> This time he asks "Peter, do you PHILEO me?"
> And Peter answers "Yes, Lord, I PHILEO you."

Read Matthew 16:13-19

Who does Peter say that Jesus is?

What does Jesus say will be true of Simon Peter?

Jesus is now making these things true. Probably not quite as Peter envisioned it. But Peter dared to search his heart. He then dared to give Jesus honest answers about what he found there. And Jesus then meets him where he's at – both literally and figuratively – and starts restoring Peter *through* his pain. *Through* his suffering. Not around it or over it or despite it. He does the same for us.

**Let's dare to be boat-jumpers, guys.
Even when it looks like boat-falling.
Let's run to meet Jesus even when
there are hard conversations ahead.**

Real quick, back to John 21:15-21

What Jesus does NOT do here may be just as important as what He DOES do. He does NOT yell at Peter, condemn Peter, or belittle Peter.

He goes to the heart. Restores Peter. And then gives him a mission.

What is Christ restoring in you?

What mission is He giving you?

A prayer for today: your words to Him

Jesus, I do marvel at you. Sometimes in celebration. Sometimes in confusion. Yet you find me. Help me "go there" with You, and trust You with the real questions and the real answers of my heart. Search me, know me, show me, lead me. And thanks for continuing the family business: You guys are really good at this restoration stuff.

A verse for today: His words to you

As a Shepherd seeks out his flock when he is among his sheep that have been scattered, so will I seek out my sheep, and I will rescue them from all the places where they have been scattered on a day of clouds and thick darkness.

– Ezekiel 34:12

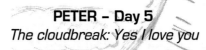

PETER – Day 5
The cloudbreak: Yes I love you

Read Isaiah 42:10-16

Sometimes God gives us a new song. Look at verses 13-15. Sometimes to create the new, the old has to be destroyed. What are the things God says He will do?

My favorite is verse 16. What are the promises God makes here?

The idea of a *new* song has always struck me. It presupposes that there is an *old song, or an original song* that we expected. And these promises are both of tearing down and building back up. That's what we've seen with Peter. God gave Peter a new song. **Sometimes He asks us to trade in our soundtracks, too.**

Is there a song God is asking you to trade in?

Read Acts 2:14-41

Compare to Luke 22:54-62
I mean, do you even recognize this guy? This is a guy with a new song.

Who did he deny Jesus in front of?

Who was he preaching to in Acts 2? (verse 14)

What was the result? [verse 41]

Read Acts 3:1-16

Look at verse 6. What does he give to the man?

Looks like somebody gave up fishing. Just sayin'.

Read 2 Peter 1:5-12

What does Peter say to add together in verses 5-7 and WHY (verse 8)?

_____ + _____ + _____ + _____

_____ + _____ + _____ + _____

SO THAT (=) _____

Okay, Greek detour time again. Because awesome-sauce.

In verse 7, the greek word used for brotherly affection is PHILEO. And the greek word for love is AGAPE. Sound familiar?

Peter, the guy who Jesus met at the seashore, the guy who Jesus restored slowly and intimately and personally, is telling us what Jesus told him. It's like Peter is saying this is what I had to be reminded of and so now I remind you. **Start with what you have, and then add.**

That day on the seashore, Peter had PHILEO. And then he added AGAPE.

What is <u>one thing</u> from the list 1 2 Peter 1:5-12 that can you offer Jesus <u>right now</u>? Be honest.

What is <u>one thing</u> you can add? Yes, one. It's overwhelming when we try to add them all, but we try to do that a lot. Sometimes that's sincere, sometimes it's a cop-out. But pick one that you can focus on adding right now. And then add more later.

But there are things that get in the way, right? For Peter too. This isn't about figuring it all out or having this perfect story. But it is about pushing through. Peter had some of the same obstacles we do.

Like **Focusing on others**

Read John 21:20-22

And here, so much love for Peter. Because he's just so real.

What does he ask Jesus here?

And what does Jesus answer?

Peter's a pretty big deal. His story is a pretty big deal. But he's still just a guy. He's still just a guy comparing himself with another guy.

So you could finish this study and just say "*wow, that was a nice story about Peter*", and just keep focusing on other people's stories OR you can hear Jesus' answer and take it as your own. **YOU follow ME**.

***But* my pesky doubt**

Read Matthew 28:16-20

The eleven disciples were at the ascension, so we know for sure this included Peter.

Look at verse 17. What were the two responses?

AFTER ALL THAT, there was still doubt. So yeah, it's pesky. But it's not powerful. Jesus is not like Santa Claus, dependent on the belief of children around the world. **Jesus is bigger than our doubts**. Bigger than denial. Bigger than hard conversations.

Doubt doesn't cancel out worship. Doubt didn't cancel Jesus' ascension. **Denial didn't end Peter's story.** The Holy Spirit still came. His Church was still built. So don't let these things cancel your story, or your part in the Church. **YOU follow HIM.**

A prayer and verse for today: your words to Him from His words to you

Based on verse 9, fill this in with **your name and make it your prayer for today**:

_____ is chosen.

_____ is a part of God's kingdom,
His holy nation, His very own possession.

This is so that _____ can show others the goodness of God,

for he called _____ out of darkness into His wonderful light.

WEEK 3 REFLECTION

Take time here to write down what you want to keep from this week. Go back through your notes and re-write things that stood out to you, what you had circled, notes that you underlined and nuggets you want to remember.

Pray for God to reveal one thing from this eek that He wants to cement deep in your heart about who He is and who you are. Remember that He who began a good work in you will be faithful to complete it.

Because God is _____

I know that I am _____

HABAKKUK – Day 1
The lightning strike: Injustice

Meet Habakkuk ...

Habakkuk is one of my favorites. Not only for his name, though I give him props for growing up with it. And not only because his book gets so easily overlooked and I love finding the hidden nuggets. But because Habakkuk is so one of my tribe-members. I mean that in the Seth Godin sense, not the tribes-of-Israel sense.

Habakkkuk is bold. He is incensed by injustice. And he is unwilling to sit silently by while things he doesn't understand happen around him. These three chapters are a conversation between Habakkuk and God – basically it's Habakkuk saying **"what the @%!& is going on here?"** *I've had those conversations too, though I can't imagine if one of them was written down for all of eternity. But I'm so glad his is, because in it we will see some amazing things about this man, and the God to whom he dares to complain. As we follow him this week, we will discover some of the same surprises that he did.*

Note: I recommend reading Habakkuk in *The New Living Translation* – I like the storytelling manner of that translation, and think it's particularly helpful with getting a picture of this conversation between God and Habakkuk.

Read Habakkuk 1:1-4

This world is a heavy place. It takes about two minutes of watching the news for me to get pretty dang depressed. The top headlines on my *BBC News App* this morning are about death, war, riots, rockets, ISIS, and bombers. Add that to the "headlines" of my friends and family – cancer, stress, divorce, miscarriage, financial worries – and it can get really sad and confusing, right?

Have you ever felt anger towards injustice burn within you? Describe such a time.

Have you ever been upset on behalf of someone else? Describe.

What are some of the "headlines" that Habakkuk is complaining about?
What does he list as things he sees happening all around him?

What are some of the "headlines" in your life right now?
Maybe directly in your life, maybe broader, even global.
Feel free to grab a newsApp if you want to list actual headlines.

Who does Habakkuk complain to?

What, specifically in verse 2, is Habakkuk asking for?

God is big enough for us to be upset with him. What I love about Habakkuk in these passages is that he is fierce. He is bold. **Why**? Because He knows God is big enough to take it. He trusts God enough to be honest with Him about how he's feeling.

Read Psalm 18:6

Write out the full verse here:

Identify something you want help from the Lord in:

But it's not just "help" that Habakkuk wants. This isn't a nice, passive request for help. He wants justice. And he's mad that he's not seeing it. He is complaining.

How is Habakkuk worshiping God in these verses?
Remember, worship means 'to show worth'.

Habakkuk dares to complain. Not to the authorities, but to THE authority. He knows that God is either sovereign over everything, or sovereign over nothing. The word 'sovereign' doesn't leave room for anything else. When you have placed your faith in God as THE authority, it can make things all the harder when you look around, like Habakkuk, and ask:

"Where the heck are you while all this injustice is going on?"
- Habakkuk

Have you ever felt that way? If so, describe.

We don't do God any favors when we hold back, as if we are trying to protect Him from how we REALLY feel.

Go ahead: tell God how you REALLY feel about _____ happening around you right now. Heck, based on today's headlines, it may even be a repeat of Habakkuk's complaints.

Read Habakkuk 1:5-11

Look at the heading above this section. What does it say?

This is the part that's often missed. Our complaints may START the conversation, **but they do not FINISH it.** The Lord replies. Let's listen.

God responds pretty specifically. And strongly. Write out the three statements that God makes in verse 5:

These are pretty amazing statements, right? I mean, these are the ones I want to hold onto forever and every day. And we should. But God continues on. What He says next is a little tougher to swallow.

Summarize what God is warning Habakkuk about in verses 6-11:

Wha????? Oh how many times do I want to cut God off at the beginning of His response. *Ok, cool, you're doing something amazing, phew.* But God tells Habakkuk that this "amazing" thing is going to come with utter destruction and devastation first.

- 92 -

Read Habakkuk 1:12-2:1

Habakkuk is reeling. *Wait, what? I come to you about injustice and you just tell me that there's* more injustice coming? And yet, we see something new in Habakkuk's posture here.

In verses 12-13, what does Habakkuk appeal to? Who does He say that God is? Write the words that he uses to describe God here

In verse 13, how does Habakkuk begin?

Based on who God is, based on God being a God of justice, how does Habakkuk now frame his question in the second half of verse 13?

I think this is the heart of Habakkuk's whole conversation. This, right here. ^ Because He can't wrap his head around how God can be one thing (i.e., Just) while other things are going on around him that defy that (i.e., could God's people be unjustly destroyed?).

He is staring down the UNGOOD
and trying to reconcile that with a GOOD God.

Friday's Rain   © Brooke Mardell, 2016, v.2

Verses 1-4 are almost more like a rant. And rants are okay. Rants are even important. Then he listens. And his response in verse 12 shows that he *really* listened; he didn't just wait for his turn to talk. By getting through the rant, Habakkuk gets to the heart. And in verses 14-17 we see a much deeper cry of his heart. He is asking "*do we mean nothing to You? Are you arbitrary in who lives and dies, like fish caught in a net?*"

When we dare to get our feelings out, and when we dare to listen to who God is, we have a chance to get to the heart of what's eating at us.

If YOU are THIS, then how is THIS happening?

Read the following verses and write how God is described in each.

Psalm 23:1   Psalm 68:5

Psalm 147:8   Isaiah 25:4

1 John 3:1   Psalm 103:3

Circle any of the above if your heart has wrestled with (or is wrestling with) this concept of God.

We can come to God with our questions, our frustrations. Questioning God can actually be a **demonstration OF faith, not a departure from it**. To question Him is to presume He will answer. (But do beware of questions that are really STATEMENTS of us knowing better than He does.)

Describe a time (maybe now) that your heart has said *Wha!?!?!?!?* as you tried to reconcile WHO God is with WHAT is happening:

Write down questions you've raised about God. Be brave. Be honest.

You guys, this isn't an exercise. This is real life. As I write this, I just got a text from a friend whose nine year old grandson has cancer. A NINE YEAR OLD WITH CANCER. This world isn't messing around. It's here to kick our butts; and we don't do ourselves or anyone else any favors when we tame our questions or pretend we aren't in the real world.

← Side-rant: we also don't do the world any favors if we don't create safe spaces to ask these questions. The Church is a place for the wounded and sick and bleeding. Side-rant over. →

> I see clearly that the thing the Church needs most today is the ability to heal wounds and to warm the hearts of the faithful; it needs nearness, proximity. I see the Church as a field hospital after battle.
> – Pope Francis

Okay, *now* side-rant over.

Now, go back to the list of who God is (one page back). **This is critical.** Because it's our anchor, just as it was Habakkuk's. From that list, choose one that you're wrestling with and ask God to reveal Himself as this in your own life. Write what you've chosen here:

Be real with yourself and God – you're both stronger than you think you are.

Because this. Look at verse 2:1. What does Habakkuk do and say here?

Take up your station.
He expects God to answer.
May we do the same.

A prayer for today: your words to Him

God, when I look around me, I sometimes get confused. There's a lot of stuff that I just don't understand. You are such a GOOD God, but there are so very many UNGOOD things happening. Please show yourself to me as I take my stand on the watchtower. I trust You to answer.

A verse for today: His words to you

If you seek it like silver and search for it as for hidden treasures, then you will understand the fear of the Lord and find the knowledge of God. – Prov. 2:4-5

HABAKKUK – Day 2
The thunder: Am I God or are you?

Read Habakkuk 2:2-20

What does God ask Habakkuk to do in verse 2:2?

This answer isn't just for Habakkuk. Not just for this moment. But for anyone passing by to read it. That's us. We are "running by" this passage this morning. Let's read the message written out.

Summarize verse 3 in your own words and write it here:

If it seems slow, wait for it ... what "seems slow" in your world right now?

What is it that we are to wait for?

→ Note: it's important to remember that God is talking about HIS vision, which isn't always the same as ours, as we'll see.

In 2:4-13, it's God's turn to rant.
Summarize what He is upset about:

So God also hates injustice. He and Habakkuk are aligned in this, and He **doarn't pretend "everything is fine,** I don't know what you're complaining about." And actually He isn't a big fan of the Chaldeans (the people He's going to use in this moment). But Israel is guilty of some of these things too.

Are there any parts of YOUR life that God might rant about?

In verse 2:14, what does God say will happen?

← THAT is His vision.

What does God compare Himself to in verses 2:18-19?

I really couldn't believe my eyes. Really. There sat the statue.

Surrounded by flowers. Incense burning.

But it was the chanting that really had me rooted in place.

Hundreds of women and men surrounded me, chanting in rythym to

… this statue. I later learned that they were, among other things,

reminding this statue to wake up the sun and bring it up over the water.

My heart broke as I watched this ritual take place.

I knew that this statue could never answer them.

Could never save them.

And had absolutely nothing to do with waking up the sun.

Look at verse 2:20

Where does God say He is while this conversation is taking place?

God reveals His king-ship several different ways throughout Scripture.

Look at 1 Timothy 6:15 and Revelation 19:16.
How does God define Himself?

Think for a minute. What would be different about your response to your life right now if you REALLY lived like God was the King?

I AM ON MY THRONE.
- **God**

Take a minute to sit in silence and ponder this. Because the conversation does continue. But only after we "sit silent before Him." Then watch for the truth of His kingship in your life.

Another way God describes Himself is as a Shepherd. It's actually the self-description God uses most.

Read Psalm 23

Who is the Shepherd?

The Lord is your Shepherd.
Which means you ain't.
- Albert Tate

What are the active verbs in this passage?
I know, grammar, GAH!

Sometimes I try to shepherd myself when I think it's all up to me. Now listen, we should be responsible for things like bills and vitamins and exercise and showing up at family birthday parties. The difference is in what we think our real responsibilities are – believing whether or not we control the outcome. That if we "do everything right", everything will turn out right. But if the Lord is my Shepherd, <u>and I ain't</u>, then I am responsible to *follow* but not to trail-blaze.

What are ways you try to "shepherd yourself"?

Read Ecclesiastes 11:5

What does it say we do not know?

You guys there are so many things we think we know. Like how babies are made. We've got charts and thermometers and smart doctors and pills and really awkward tests. But we still don't know the work of God who makes everything. Including babies. And that's okay.

- 100 -

Read John 10:10-15

We have an enemy. What does he seek to do?

In other words: wreak havoc and injustice.

How does Jesus describe Himself?

And what is His purpose as the Good Shepherd?

**The Lord is our Shepherd, so we ain't.
Let this be a promise to you today.
You ain't the Shepherd.
You ain't the boss.
You ain't on the throne.**

A prayer for today: your words to Him

God, I want to live like you are my Shepherd. Like You are my King. Like You are on the throne. Please show me what that looks like today.

A verse for today: His words to you

My sheep hear my voice, and I know them, and they follow me. I give them eternal life, and they will never perish, and no one will snatch them out of my hand. – John 10:27

HABAKKUK – Day 3
The storm gear: Watch and See

Read Habakkuk 1:5

God tells Habakkuk He will be surprised at what He does –
"I'm doing something you wouldn't understand even if I explained it to you."

Pause and think back. Are there things that you could see God doing only in hindsight? Any ways that God has surprised you before? List them here.

Read Habakkuk 3:2

What is Habakkuk doing in this verse?

Identify what he says in this verse about the past, present, and future.

Past:

Present:

Future:

Part of the future is the past and the present.
Part of watching is remembering.

Read 1 Chron. 16:8-36

What word appears in both verses 12 and 15?

→ **The word remember** appears over 150 times in Scripture. ←

What are they remembering in this passage?

Read Isaiah 63:7-14

In verse 7, what is being remembered?

Read Psalm 103:1-5

What are we to "forget not"?

What are the "benefits" the Psalmist identifies in verses 3-5?

**Sometimes we don't find comfort from what lies ahead,
but from what lies behind.**

Following the lead of Habakkuk, Isaiah, and the Psalmist, spend some time in remembrance. Identify times you have seen God at work, even if you didn't understand it as it was happening.

Where do you see God in your Past:

Where do you see God in your Present:

Where are you watching for God in your Future:

What is one benefit from Psalm 103:1-5 you want to hold onto today:

A prayer for today: your words to Him

God, I want to be amazed and surprised at what You are doing. Help me to remember the things You have already done in the past – in my past – as I look to the future and wonder what You will be doing next. I know You might not explain it all to me. Help me understand. Help me remember.

A verse for today: His words to you

I will not forget you. Behold, I have engraved you on the palms of my hands.
- Isaiah 49:15b-16a

HABAKKUK –
The path: Patience

**God's aim looks like missing the
mark because we are too
short-sighted to see
what He is aiming at.**
– Oswald Chambers

Does this sound familiar much!?

Look at Habakkuk 3:3. Then **read Deuteronomy 33:1-4.**
What is Habakkuk referring to in 3:3?

Look at Habakkuk 3:5. Then **review Exodus 7:14-10:29.**
What is Habakkuk referring to here?

Look at Habakkuk 3:8-15. Then **read Exodus 14.**
Then give Habakkuk a virtual high-five for capturing
this story of the Red Sea so poetically.

Look at verses 8 and 13 again in Habakkuk 3. WAS GOD MAD AT THE WATER
WHEN HE PARTED THE RED SEA? OR WAS HE RESCUING HIS PEOPLE?
[*Yes this question has to be in all caps because holy-HOLINESS!*]

In Exodus 14, we read the story from Moses' and Israel's perspective – what
they experienced. In Habakkuk 3:8-15 we read the story from the perspective of
what God was doing. Habakkuk is remembering a time where **it could have
looked like God was arbitrarily destroying people.** But He
was actually on a rescue mission.

The God of the Bible is the God of rescue. By remembering the days of old, who God is, Habakkuk is answering his own questions from Chapter 1.

Compare Habakkuk 3 to Habakkuk 1:1-4 and 12-17
What is different about how Habakkuk is addressing God now?

Look back at the questions you wrote down on day 1 of this week. Have they changed in any way? If so, re-write them here. If not, keep asking them. He will answer you.

As Habakkuk went from making a plea to expressing patience, we now see him entering into praise. **Amidst the confusion, not after it.** He joins his voice with those who have gone before and come after, saying "You are the God who rescues." And, also like those who have gone before, he's learning that rescue might look different than he'd imagined.

Read Daniel 6

In verses 1-13, a political plot unfolds. Daniel is put in the middle of injustice. Identify the ways that justice was perverted in this story:

Describe a time that you felt like injustice got the best of a situation:

In verses 16-25, who is transformed the most?

I've always heard this story as Daniel being rescued from lions. And there's that too. And it's awesome. **But I think it's also the story of King Darius being rescued**. Rescued from politics and fears and injustice that he found himself wrapped up in. And ultimately, rescued INTO a faith in the true God.

In verses 26-27, write out how King Darius describes the God of Daniel:

Circle the first line from verse 27. He delivers and rescues. But sometimes that involves time in the Lion's Den.

Read 2 Timothy 4:16-17

Who does Paul identify as the one who stood by and strengthened him?

What does Paul say he was rescued from in verse 17?

Habakkuk was crying out from his own Lion's Den. You may be crying out from a Lion's Den. Take heart. He is a God of rescue. But who and what and how He's rescuing doesn't always make sense to us. And sometimes wouldn't even if He explained it to us. Because even while He's closing the mouths of a lion, He may be opening the heart of a King.

A prayer for today: your words to Him

Read Psalm 71

This is the cry of David's heart from his "lion's den". Pick a verse from this passage that speaks the cry of YOUR heart today, maybe one of plea, patience, praise, or somewhere in between. Write it out here, and then tell someone else that this is your prayer today.

A verse for today: His words to you

I will rescue you from every evil deed and bring you safely home into my heavenly kingdom.

– 2 Timothy 4:18a

HABAKKUK – Day 5
The cloudbreak: Resolve of Praise

IF YOU NEVER EVER EVER EVER GIVE ME WHAT I WANT, I'LL PRAISE YOU.
- Habakkuk

Read Habakkuk 3:17-19

These are his final words. We're gonna camp here today. I hope you can camp here even longer. These words of praise carry more authenticity than most prayers or sermons I've ever heard.

Did Habakkuk's situation change?

Was Habakkuk given any promise that he'd get what he wanted?

Look up these passages and write down what IS promised in each verse:

Psalm 119:58

Acts 2:37-39

2 Peter 3:13

1 John 2:25

Read 2 Cor. 1:19-20

In Jesus, the promises of God find what?

Check one. ❑   Yes   ❑   No

The divine yes. **Hear this**.

Every time that you hear
Does God really love me/care about me/save me/keep His promises?
YES!

God's promises + Jesus = YES

Now, here's where things can get tricky when we confuse the promise of WHO God is with WHAT we expect Him to do. We trade the ACTUAL promises of God for what we wish His promises were.

Countless Christians have fallen prey to this idea that faith means getting the results you want. Verses about God's faithfulness and us having faith the size of a mustard seed have led to heartbreaking moments where someone feels like the results they're experiencing is their fault, because they don't have enough faith. But if our faith is in results, we'll never have "enough". **Faith in results will always leave us empty.**

Read Hebrews 11

This passage is often referred to as "the hall of faith".

How is faith defined in verse 1?

List the people identified by name in this "hall of faith" in verses 1-3

Now look at verse 13. Did all of these people receive the things promised?

They saw the promise from afar. Interesting. We get this glimpse that not all promises are fulfilled in this one life span. Not all are fulfilled this side of heaven.

List some of the results of faith you see in verses 33-34:

Now list some of the results of faith you see in verses 35-38

Tough, right? **Both** of these lists were results of faith. Let me say again: **both of these lists were results of faith.** Some stopped the mouths of lions, others were fed to the mouths of lions. *What on earth*!?

But see, Jesus is more real with us than we often are with each other. He never promised results. I often wish He had. I wish He had promised me a baby. He didn't. I wish He had promised you a husband. He didn't. I wish He promised us health and wealth. He doesn't. And it's okay to want the comfort and the joy and all the good feels. I celebrate that my life is filled with so many. But He doesn't promise those. He promises something more.

Read Romans 8:31-39

List the things that can seem to stand against Christ's love in verses 35, 38-39?

Circle any of the things on that list that YOU have experienced or are experiencing.

What is the promise that stands up against tribulation, distress, persecution, famine, nakedness, danger, sword, death, life, angels, rulers, things present, things to come, powers, height, depth, and ANYTHING ELSE EVER EVER EVER?

You are loved.
You are loved.
You are loved.
THAT is my promise.
- Jesus

Read Romans 9:24-26

What will God call us?

You are the Beloved. Your only job is to **Be. Loved.**

Habakkuk taught me that the end of the story is just the beginning.

That one story ends and another begins at the point of surrender.

We didn't start here because, well, because we can't start here. I don't believe that Habakkuk could have said the words of 3:17-19 without walking through the rest of the conversation with God. I don't believe we can either.

And surrender isn't a one-time experience. It has sequels.

Once upon a time I surrendered ...
... and then another time.
... and then another time.
... and then another time.

You started something tonight. Something real, raw and painful. Or maybe it's

something you started a long time ago. Something I can't even identify as the beginning,

the end, or betwixt. What I know is that my raised hands literally shook as my tears fell tonight,

because for the first time, I envisioned the baby I've always wanted to hold – the way my hands

were raised, I could have been supporting a wee baby butt and a wee baby head.

But my hands were empty. Being held up to You in surrender.

Have I fully let go of the baby I always thought these hands would hold?

I don't know. Can one? I don't know. What I know is that I experienced

physical pain, as something (or someone?) was rooted from my heart

in surrender – or at least the beginning of surrender. March 4, 2012

Fill in Habakkuk 3:17-19 with your empty places in which you are learning to praise Him.

DO NOT fill in these blanks until your heart means it. Empty words are like a clanging cymbal. I don't say that with judgment but with freedom. Don't just make noise here. Even if it means putting this book down and coming back to it days, weeks or months from now, don't offer this prayer to God until you can really mean it. And if that day is not today, then pray for this to become true in your heart. **He who hears you is faithful. He will complete** what He has started in you.

THOUGH _____ SHOULD NOT BLOSSOM, NOR

_____ BE ON THE VINES, THE PRODUCE OF

_____ FAIL, AND _____ YIELD NO

_____, THE FLOCK BE CUT OFF FROM THE FIELD, AND NO

_____, YET WILL I REJOICE IN THE LORD; I WILL

TAKE JOY IN THE GOD OF MY SALVATION; GOD, THE LORD, IS MY STRENGTH,

HE MAKES MY FEET LIKE THE DEER'S; HE MAKES ME TREAD ON MY HIGH

PLACES.

*Here's my example – it took me a few **years** to mean it,*
so, you know, go your own speed:

THOUGH **MY WOMB** SHOULD NOT BLOSSOM, NOR **A BABY EVER** BE ON THE VINES, THE PRODUCE OF **FERTILITY TREATMENTS** FAIL, AND **MY ATTEMPTS** YIELD NO **BABY WITH MY HUSBAND'S EYES**, THE FLOCK BE CUT OFF FROM THE FIELD, AND NO **BABY IN A CRADLE - EVER**, YET WILL I REJOICE IN THE LORD; I WILL TAKE JOY IN THE GOD OF MY SALVATION; GOD, THE LORD, IS MY STRENGTH, HE MAKES MY FEET LIKE THE DEER'S; HE MAKES ME TREAD ON MY HIGH PLACES.

Also, go read **HINDS FEET ON HIGH PLACES, by Hannah Hurnard.** You'll thank me later.

A prayer for today: your words to Him

God, I want this prayer to be true of my heart. That whatever comes – or doesn't come – I could praise You. Teach me to be the Beloved. Teach me to be loved. Be my strength, be my joy, and take me to the High Places.

A verse for today: His words to you

I forgive all your sins,
I heal all your diseases;

I redeem your life from the pit,
I crown you lavishly with lovingkindness and tender mercy;

I satisfy your years with good things,
So that your youth is renewed like the soaring eagle.

- Psalm 103:3-5 (AMP)

WEEK 4 REFLECTION

Take time here to write down what you want to keep from this week. Go back through your notes and re-write things that stood out to you, what you had circled, notes that you underlined and nuggets you want to remember.

Pray for God to reveal one thing from this eek that He wants to cement deep in your heart about who He is and who you are. Remember that He who began a good work in you will be faithful to complete it.

Because God is _____

I know that I am _____

MARTHA – Day 1
The lightning strike: Unanswered Prayer

Meet Martha ...

... Lord bless it, Martha has gotten a bad rap. We are told not to be 'Marthas'. To have a peaceful Mary heart in a world full of busy-bee Marthas because of THAT STORY where Martha was hot and bothered that her sister was sitting at Jesus' feet instead of helping her in the kitchen. But you guys, I gotta tell you, I'm rather hoping I CAN be a 'Martha' in this world, and I think you'll see why when we're done with this week.

Martha will be one of the first I want to get tea with in heaven someday. Loose-leaf, of course - the only tea I can imagine heaven having. Her heart was honest, confident, and faith-FULL. But Martha's heart was also broken. We will walk with her through a season of sending for her Savior, suffering in sorrow, and standing in shock.

We will get to see Jesus as she did, and in so doing, will get another glimpse of how He sees us ...

Read John 11:1-5

Who do Martha and Mary send for when their brother gets sick?

How does verse 5 describe how Jesus felt about Mary and Martha?

How do the sisters describe Lazarus to Jesus in verse 3?

Have you ever thought of your prayers to Jesus as talking to Him about someone He loves? I love that imagery. It has come to inform my prayers in meaningful and powerful ways.

Think of someone you're praying for right now – or who has asked you for prayer. If no one immediately comes to mind, hop on Facebook – I can bet you a dollar there's someone in your feed asking for prayer.

Write a prayer for them here that starts with "Lord, _____, whom you love, is _____".

And may all our prayers be so personal. May we trust, as Martha did, that Jesus loves those we are talking to Him about.

Write out **Jeremiah 31:3b** here.

That everlasting love is also yours, my friend.

Back to John 11.
In verse 4, what is Jesus' response to the news that Lazarus is ill?
What does He say will NOT happen?
What does He say WILL happen?

Pause. We aren't told whether or not Jesus sent Martha a response. But there's a good chance that someone somewhere said something like "**Jesus says he'll be fine.**" Which, honestly, seems like a fair interpretation. If you were Martha and got that response, what would you expect? How would you feel?

Have you ever had a moment where you felt like God said everything would be ok? Or where someone else said "*God told me this is going to be ok*"? If so, describe. Try to identify how it made you feel and what it made you think about God.

Also, we often bring our own definition to "ok".
Just hold onto that nugget for a minute.

Read John 11:6, 14

Anyone else feel like we just took a left turn? Like Jesus hit the snooze button in the middle of an emergency? Try and put yourself in Martha's shoes for a second. What happened to Lazarus? What does Jesus say plainly in verse 14?

So he knew.

We've all felt the sting of unanswered prayer. And by 'unanswered' we usually mean we didn't get the answer we wanted. Look closely at verse 6. What did Jesus do when he heard the prayer of Martha and Mary?

Have you ever felt like Jesus heard your prayer and then basically did … nothing? Describe a time you've felt like that. Like God was silent in response to a prayer:

If you stopped reading here, what would you think about Jesus?

A lot of people stop reading here. Not literally stop reading. But a lot of people choose to be done with Jesus when they feel like their prayers were to no avail. Because OF COURSE this is confusing and weird. We're told Jesus loves them. And then instead of racing to their side, he gets news that Lazarus is sick and He does …. nothing. For two days. We're told Jesus loves us. But too many feel like that love is on pause for much longer than two days. Some stop reading here. But we won't.

Take time to reflect on any areas of your life where an 'unanswered' prayer has made you want to 'stop reading'.

A prayer for today: your words to Him

God, I don't want to stop reading, stop watching, and stop counting on you even when it's really confusing to see You doing, well, nothing sometimes. At least nothing I can see. It really hurts when I pray and it doesn't feel like You answer. Help me to "keep reading" in those moments.

A verse for today: His words to you

I don't take naps on the job.

- Psalm 121:2

MARTHA – Day 2
The thunder: Do you know who I am?

We will keep reading. Because the story is far from over.

Read John 11:7-16

In these verses it's like we get to go behind-the-scenes for a moment. The stage turns just a bit and we steal a glance behind the curtain. And we hear a conversation that is about a much bigger script than what we saw playing out on stage.

What does Jesus suggest in verse 7?

What is his disciples response in verse 8?

What reason does Jesus give for wanting to go back to Judea? (verse 11)

How do the disciples interpret that? Do they think it's really necessary that Jesus go to Judea? (verses 12-13)

Then in verse 14 Jesus gets plain. "You guys, he's not asleep. He's dead." And in verse 15 He offers a more personal reason that they need to go now. What reason does he give?

Look back at 11:4. What reason did Jesus give there as to Lazarus' illness?

I don't like this verse. Well really, I don't like how it gets mis-used in its re-telling. I can't count how many times I've heard people dismiss someone's suffering with a statement like "God must need the glory". Stop. Just stop. God does not *need* the glory. He is worth glory, He personifies glory, He has glory, and He can bring glory in and out of every.single.thing but He is not so weak that He needs to cause suffering here for His glory there. Gross. Also, this passage doesn't suggest that God causes illness so that He will get glory. It says this one was for that purpose. **Please be careful about ascribing God's glory to someone's pain.** Please don't be gross.

So when I say that a bigger script is unfolding, I'm not suggesting that Lazarus and Martha and Mary were just collateral damage that God shrugged off because He would get glory out of it. In fact, one of the most intimate verses of all of Scripture is coming up soon – and sometimes I wonder whether that's the part that's even more glorious than what we see with Lazarus and the tomb. But I'm getting ahead of myself.

I'm saying that this behind-the-scenes-look hits pause on Lazarus to give us context about Jesus' Messiah-ship (Messiah-ship could be a word).

What do the Disciples think will happen once they return? (verse 16)

They weren't exactly paranoid. Their fears were well-founded.

Read John 10:22-40

In verse 31, what do the Jews do in response to Jesus?

In verse 33, what do they give as their reason for wanting to kill Jesus?

In verse 24, what started all this? What do the Jews ask of Jesus?

Christ is the same word used for Messiah. The Jewish people had been waiting for their Messiah, their Savior, since he was first predicted to Adam and Eve. Their rabbis kept track of predictions about Messiah, and all the ways they would recognize Him when He came.

They had met false prophets, false Messiahs. They were on their guard. They had asked these questions of others. But they had never received these answers before. Problem is, they were unwilling to hear and see them. Which, ironically, was also one of the predictions (Isaiah 6:9).

One of the ways they were told they'd recognize the Messiah was that the blind would receive their sight.

Read John 9

What happens in verses 7-11?

- 126 -

Who questions him in verses 13-17? What questions do they ask?

What is their response in verse 18?

In verses 24-34, it's almost as if we get to witness an internal struggle within the minds of the Pharisees. What are their questions focused on?

What does the man-once-blind focus his answers on?

In verses 35-38, who does Jesus identify Himself as?

Have you ever **focused more on your questions than God's answers?** It's easy to do. Take a minute and ask God if, like the Pharisees, there are answers you're hearing but not hearing. Or don't want to hear the answer about. Really listen. And write down anything He gives you:

Now take time to experience him as the once-blind-man did, **and dare to give his answers.** He doesn't try to explain the things he can't explain, but he is bold and direct about the things he DOES know ("I was blind. Now I see.") Write down the things that you know about God working in your life, without worrying about the parts you can't explain:

Read John 8:53-59

What do the Jews do in verse 59?

What was the statement that Jesus made just before that? What incited them? (verse 58)

What are the two questions the Jews ask in verse 53?

- 128 -

Jesus brought sight to the blind.

Declared Himself equal with God.

And said He was there before Abraham.

It's almost funny that they even asked "are you the Messiah"?

But they didn't think it was funny.

They are at war within themselves as to Who he is.

And they've decided that one more statement as Messiah will be His last.

Back to **John 11:16**

So the disciples weren't exactly exaggerating when they said that death awaited them. They had already narrowly escaped it multiple times. They had already declared Him Messiah, whatever the cost.

The once-blind-man had a chance to declare Jesus as Messiah.

The Disciples had a chance to declare Jesus as Messiah.

The Pharisees had a chance to declare Jesus as Messiah.

Soon Martha would have her chance to declare Him Messiah.

And hers would also come at a great cost.

A prayer for today: your words to Him

There are days I have lot of questions too. Please give me the eyes of the blind man and not of the Pharisees so I can see you for who you really are.

A verse for today: His words to you

But who do you say that I am?

- Matthew 16:15

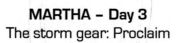

MARTHA – Day 3
The storm gear: Proclaim

Read John 11:17-27

When does Jesus arrive? How long had Lazarus been in the tomb?

What does Martha do in verse 20?

> *Isn't it sad that Martha is known for her hot-mess-kitchen-faux-pax and not for this moment? Sometimes we do that to each other, too. Or ourselves. We hold onto the "oops" moment as an identity piece.*

What does she express to Jesus in verse 21 and 22?

In verse 23, what is Jesus' response?

In verse 24, how does she interpret that?

This was a girl who had studied.
This was a girl who had made her own choices to believe.

Write down what Martha says in verse 27.

I love this woman for her solid and bold theology. **She knows who Jesus is.** She goes to Him. I don't know what her tone was here: one of anger or acceptance? The words could go either way. And maybe that's not the important part. But she is declaring Him as the Christ, the One who saves, *after* her brother has died. *After* she heard silence in response to her request for Lazarus' healing. *After* she had reason to doubt, she chose to proclaim Him as Messiah.

It's a beautiful picture of faith, because we live in the same world that Martha does. Where people die. **People that love Jesus and are loved by Jesus.** We can stare into the face of the Ungood without losing sight of who God is. This is not easy. But it is critical.

Martha's faith is highlighted here up against the backdrop of the scene unfolding between Jesus and the Jewish leaders. Throughout the Old Testament, the Jewish leaders are described as 'the Shepherds of Israel', entrusted to lead and guide the Marthas and the Marys and the Lazaruses of their communities to God. Where the Jewish Leaders had failed to lead Martha to the Messiah, we see that she was nonetheless found by Him. Because He is the Good Shepherd. In fact, that's part of the very battle playing in the background.

Read John 10:1-19
In verses 1-5, what analogy does Jesus give?

This is still in response to the opening-the-eyes-of-the-blind-man-fiasco. We know that because verse 21 says their internal conflict is that they can't (won't?) reconcile the words Jesus is saying with what they just saw when he healed a blind man.

In verses 11 and 14, what does Jesus call Himself?

In verses 12-13, what does Jesus compare to?
What are the poor qualities of a hired hand that Jesus identifies?

What are the qualities of a Good Shepherd that Jesus identified in verses 11 and 14?

This wasn't a new conversation. In fact, it had been set up centuries before. Jesus often used terms and analogies that would be familiar to Jewish teachers and leaders. He made references that they would recognize and connect to texts they had studied all their life. It's a little bit how I could say "I pledge allegiance to the flag ... " and my fellow Americans would instantly hear the rest of the Pledge in their mind. Because it's something they learned in grade school, it's ingrained. Often the words Jesus used, while powerful as a stand-alone, were even more powerful when recognized as a spark that was igniting a bigger conversation.

Read Ezekiel 34:1-6

A prophecy against the Shepherds of Israel. Ouch. Those chosen to lead Israel are called out as ones who have cared for themselves instead. For our purposes here, we won't spend a lot of time dwelling on the failures of Israel's leaders, but it is well documented that the Jewish leadership that Jesus was speaking to in John 10 was full of corruption, self-dealing, and perhaps a bit drunk on power. As the Shepherds of Israel, they had fulfilled this prophecy of feeding themselves and leaving the flock weak.

- 132 -

Read Ezekiel 34:11-16

Write out verse 11:

How does God describe Himself? (verse 12)

How many times does He say a version of "*I myself, I will ...* " in this passage:

List the things that it says He himself will do:

Look at verse 12. How is the day described from which we will be rescued?

Take heart, my friend, if the day is
full of clouds and thick darkness.
Your Shepherd is near.

Back to John 11:27

Martha's declaration here is a picture of what faith can look like in the midst of pain. On a day of clouds and thick darkness. On a day of rain. Yes, Lord, I believe. Smack dab in the middle of all my feels.

But sometimes it's real tricky to find the words for that. I like borrowing from David. The Psalms offer some of the most poetic proclamations of who God is in the midst of varied emotions. I love this project because David saw – and said – it all. He has walked the high and the low and the in-between. He's a great guy to borrow a few words from.

Take a blank piece of paper. Maybe in your journal, maybe a sketch-book, maybe the next page, maybe the back of a receipt. Whatever.

Grab a pen.

Open your Bible to the Psalms. Any place is fine. You're going to roam. Wander. Explore. Just let your eyes scan over the words of the Psalms.

When words stand out to you – when your eyes land on something that your heart is trying to express – write it down. Don't think too hard about it, just respond. Just write.

You may find that David's words unlock your own. Feel free to add lines or verses.

After a time, sit back and read through Your Psalm. This is your voice of worship today. Whether it's full of praise or lament or (like many) a bit of both, it's worship when you take it to God, because it is a way of displaying Him *worthy* of coming to. It's your way of echoing the voices of centuries. Of David. Of Habakkuk. Of Martha.

A prayer for today: your psalm to Him

MARTHA – Day 4
The path: Despite common-sense

Read John 11:27, 38-39

What does Jesus say to do? (verse 38)

What does Martha say to Jesus?

This is literally one of my favorite passages of all of Scripture.
Because some of my prayers may or may not go the same way ...

"Umm, hey there, Messiah, Master, CREATOR OF ALL LIVING
THINGS ... *did you know that dead people stink?*
I'm just sayin', you might want to take that into account with this
whole stone-rolling thing you're about to do here.
I'm just here to help. You're welcome."

Me and Martha. We are so soul sisters.

Her theology is still strong. It's only been nine verses, after all. She still knows who the Messiah is. **But her common-sense is strong too.** And I love her. Because she is all of us. She is every woman who has gone to Jesus and meant every single word of praise. And then turns around and runs head-first into her common-sense. Where the impossible remains, well, impossible. She's just being practical.

- 136 -

Do you ever "remind" Jesus that "dead people stink"? Or how to do math? Or how the doctor explained the cancer to you, just so, you know, He "understands"? Describe a time that you've tried to "help" the Messiah by offering him some of your common-sense.

We do this in small things too, you guys.
And don't worry, we're in good company.
And even better, **common-sense hasn't stopped Jesus before**.
And it won't now.

Read Mark 8:1-17

What does Jesus do in verses 1-10?

In verses 14-16, what are the disciples talking about?

What had they just seen Jesus do? Literally just hours before?

How many people did Jesus feed with seven loaves of bread?

How many people were complaining they only had one loaf amongst them?

What does Jesus ask them in verse 17?

Our common-sense will always make us talk about the one loaf.
Forget about the seven and what Jesus has just done with those.
But what will we say when we hear Jesus asking
"why are you talking about the one loaf of bread?"

Describe a "seven loaf" moment you've seen.
A moment you saw God do something 'against the odds':

Describe a "one loaf" moment you've had.
Where you wonder how on earth God
is going to come through even though
you may have just seen Him do so?

How can you bring a seven-loaf perspective to this one-loaf moment?

Now back to our Martha.

Read John 11:27, 40-44

I know, *I know*. I've made you read verse 27 so many times. But it is so important that we get this. Her faith and her common-sense co-existed. And Jesus answered both in grace and power.

What does Jesus DO after Martha's statement?

And what does Jesus say to her directly in verse 40?

What does Jesus say in verse 42?

Our common-sense is not a bad thing. We shouldn't hide it. But we also shouldn't hide IN it. Jesus doesn't condemn Martha for her common-sense ... after all, dead people really do stink ... but He does offer her something more. He offers her a miracle. And I think sometimes we try and match our prayers to our common-sense. Maybe sometimes as if we have to be sure we ask for something "realistic." My friends, may we never pray as ones entitled to a miracle. But may we always pray for more than common.

A prayer for today: your words to Him

Jesus, I confess that sometimes my common-sense tells me that you need my help. Sometimes I like to think that you need me. But honestly it's more amazing that you <u>want</u> me. And my heart. And my common-sense. And all the jumbled in-between that makes me one hot mess that you love. Thank you for being the God of both the common and the miraculous. Of both the seven-loaf moments and the one-loaf moments.

A verse for today: His words to you

I am in your midst, a mighty one who will save. I will rejoice over you with gladness; I will quiet you with my love; I will exult over you with loud singing.
                                                                                    – Zephaniah 3:17

MARTHA – Day 5
The cloudbreak: Life from Loss

Oh you guys. This moment. I can't even.

Re-Read John 11:38-44

LAZARUS. COMES. OUT. OF. THE. TOMB.

I imagine Martha did a jig.
I imagine she still might every time she re-tells this story.

I know because I've danced a similar jig.

The story on the next two pages is still being written. It started in my husband's ICU room just weeks before this edition went to print, so it's a last-minute add-in, but I want to share it with you here because **it is the summation of everything I know to be true of my God**: that he doesn't HAVE to do anything, but He CAN do anything. Absolutely anything.

The last hundred hours have been the most unreal, surreal, and at the same time vividly-raw-real of my life. .
In the last hundred hours, a fierce, brutal, powerful tale of redemption and resurrection has unfolded in these hospital walls.
One still very much being written, with many questions yet unanswered, yet infused with miraculously answered prayers.

At five o'clock on Friday night, I got "the call" – the one I've dreaded with every story of Jenny Lee's Alec, Mary
Crawley's Matthew, and Meredith Shepherd's Derek. All at once, I was in my own tv drama nightmare, complete with the
perfect morning together preceding it. As a friend drove me to the hospital, I learned only bits and pieces –
CPR had been performed at the scene, he was in the cardio department awaiting a "procedure",
and the procedure could not wait and needed my consent over the phone – ending with a promise they would
"do everything they could." I'd never heard words that struck more terror ...

I had no idea how many more terrifying words would come to my ears that very night.

When we finally arrived, we waited. In silent agony and with the ER admission nurses avoiding
my direct gaze as they asked me to wait for the social worker. I met the men who had
performed CPR, the men who had used an AED at the scene. I listened as one might read a newspaper –
distant, cautious, as if about a country far away. At last I was taken back to meet a doctor – my husbands cardiologist.
The words didn't go together in my mind. He had no heart trouble, no forewarning signs, no family history of heart issues.

Nonetheless, I was told he'd had a heart attack, and had 100% blockage of an artery. They had put in a stent. He was in recovery.
And the doctor had "seen people make full recoveries" from these types of attacks, though brain activity was a large unknown.
Someone had pulled up a wheelchair; I found myself accepting it.

An hour or so later, after he was stable, they led me back to see him. As I arrived at the door to his room, I saw the tubes, the
monitors, the wires, the hospital gown. **And then the monitor flashed a red zero.** And the light above his door flashed blue.
And nurses and doctors from every direction came running as I became an extra in my own episode of Greys Anatomy.
Jason coded twelve times that night.

I can't put into words the terror of each one, or the ring of words like "flatline", "paddles – clear!" being within earshot, and being
about the man I love. My prayers were fervent and clear: life, breath, life, breath. Yet life and breath were the most elusive
things of the evening. I watched nurses work tirelessly. Doggedly. Fighting death back only to have it come running at them again.
And again. And again. At some point, I became aware that their efforts were more for me than for him – that they were doing
everything in their power to show me that they had done everything in their power. I stared at the love of my life as he stared blankly
at the ceiling, while machines kept his body alive. **I knew to sing.** I don't know how or why I knew that.
But I knew to sing over him. Hymns and songs of worship, praise, and a promise – to him and to
me – that I would declare God is good. In the shadow. Songs that defied what the eyes could see
even as it was breaking my heart in half to think what it would mean to keep
worshiping in a world without my Jason.

At 5:30am on Saturday February 20, 2016, I was told that I would soon be a widow. That there was nothing left they could do. That he was on one hundred percent life support, and that time would make no difference. **That it was time to say goodbye.** I heard a wail. A deep guttural moan filled with pain. I realized it was coming from my own mouth.

And even as my mouth said the words goodbye, even as my hands caressed the skin not covered in needles and wires, even as my mind recognized that I would never see him again this side of heaven, my heart refused for it to be true. As the doctor walked in, I told him I had only one question. My tear-soaked eyes begged him to tell me why more time wouldn't make a difference; why we weren't giving him a chance to fight. His eyes filled with discomfort, and he squirmed with the truth of what he had to tell me. That there was almost zero chance that time would make any difference at all. I clung to almost.

He agreed to wait a few more hours. I knew even then that it was merely to give me the confidence that we had tried. I took each step in a hollow fog, understanding each one was leading me to my unwanted new chapter of life as the former Mrs. Jason Miller.

One hour later, he woke up.
He. Woke. Up.

He was responsive. Answering to his name and simple commands. **The doctor couldn't explain it.** The nurse grabbed my hand and said "I've never seen anything like this!" as she raced me down the hall to his side. His still unfocused eyes started searching as he heard my voice. My hand went to his forehead and my heart leapt in hope. He was awake. He was also incredibly unstable, and I was rushed out as quickly as I was rushed in, as doctors realized that stimulation was causing his blood pressure to plummet and his heart to race erratically. Still, he had woken up. Against all odds. Life had returned to the room. And so began **a delicate vigil**, a teetering dance around vital signs and organ failure and shallow breaths and v-tachy spikes and bodily tremors and countless medications and machines. So continued a battle of heavenly proportions, where prayer requests went out around the world and loved ones flew in from around the world. Where we saw every odd beaten and every prayer answered. Where I have learned more about love than ever before as we've been surrounded these twilight and daylight hours alike.

Where life has returned. **Resurrected life.**

Today ended the dependence on drugs and machines. Even now we are beginning the weaning from sedation. With it remain many unknowns, and I keep receiving warning that we have a long road ahead, to which I say "AMEN it's long!" The short one would have ended with a funeral. But we, we are living the long road of a miracle.

Sometimes we get to the end of ourselves. Sometimes we get to the end of medicine. Sometimes we see the miracle. Sometimes we don't. I don't really have any answers for why those *sometimes* can be so different from each other.

But I know the stories in Scripture are still being written today.

And I know the stories there teach us to sing in the shadow.

And to ask without ceasing.

And to bless the name of a God who both gives and takes away.

Circle one of those four phrases that God is emphasizing to you right now. Write out a response to it:

And you guys, there's even more glory in this story.

Read John 11:28-37

We're gonna camp on verse 35 here. Two of the most powerful words in all of Scripture. Write them here:

- 144 -

What does this tell you about Jesus?

Look at verse 32. Now we see Mary coming to His feet.
What does she do?

What does Jesus see in verse 33?

How does verse 33 describe his reaction to what He sees?

How can this inform your prayers as you bring Jesus your heartaches?

I wish we made more room for weeping at Church.
It should be the **safest place of all** to bring our tears.
Maybe it would be if we realized that Jesus weeps alongside us.

- 145 -

Jesus told his Disciples that they would see the glory of God on display here. He told Martha she would see His glory here. And YES amen we see it in Lazarus, you know, WALKING OUT OF THE TOMB. But also we see it here. In the tenderness of Jesus. In his tears. He cries with us, you guys. In this is Glory.

And because there's nothing God wastes, we see Martha's story connected to that bigger script again as those watching take note of what they're witnessing.

Read John 11:45-53

In verses 45 and 46, what are the two responses described?

In verses 47-53, we see a final choice made: some to faith and life, others to fear and death. And the Shepherds of Israel: well they chose to kill Jesus. They had no idea that they were about to become one of the many predictions made about the Good Shepherd.

Where Habakkuk showed us what it looks like to **praise without answers**, Martha shows us to **always ask**. Always.

And Jesus shows us that He is **Good**.

Both when He says **no**,

And when He says **yes**.

We live in the both-and, you guys. In the now and not yet. In a world where **people die** and tragedies are made new everyday. But also in a world where **miracles still happen**. Both sides of these realities call us to a level of **bravery** that defies human comprehension and goes beyond our human strength.

Just weeks after my Jason's life was restored, one of our dearest (and most talented) friends penned and performed this amazing anthem calling us all to be brave. Please do yourself the tedious favor of typing this into a web browser and watching this Spoken Word since you can't link to it from a piece of paper.

https://willowcreek.tv/sermons/south-barrington/2016/03/give-yourself-away/#top
And click on the "Be Brave" link

Also, since you're tediously typing anyways, enter this bad boy into your browser if you want to hear my husband's testimony **in his own words**. There also might be a jig.

http://www.brookemardell.com/2016/03/30/we-are-living-a-miracle-teamjasonmiller-live/

**May we be brave, you guys.
May we sing in the shadow.
May we dance jigs to His glory.**

A prayer for today: your words to Him

Jesus, please take only what you must.
And please give everything you're willing to give.

A verse for today: His words to you

Before you call, I will answer; while you are still speaking, I will hear.
- Isaiah 65:24

WEEK 5 REFLECTION

Take time here to write down what you want to keep from this week. Go back through your notes and re-write things that stood out to you, what you had circled, notes that you underlined and nuggets you want to remember.

Pray for God to reveal one thing from this eek that He wants to cement deep in your heart about who He is and who you are. Remember that He who began a good work in you will be faithful to complete it.

Because God is _____

I know that I am _____

- 149 -

US – Day 1
From Moses: Don't Go Back to Egypt

By daring to pick up this book, you have declared yourself more than a storm-watcher. You know that sitting under the umbrella to wait it out won't get you anywhere.

Like Moses, you have dared to go *into* your pain, in a search for true freedom. Like the Two on the road to Emmaus, you have sought Christ when You couldn't see Him. Like Peter, you had the guts to search the depths of your heart, and give honest answers to honest questions. Like Habakkuk, you haven't stayed silent. And like Martha, you haven't stopped believing – even if your common sense still chimes in now and then.

You have shown bravery and strength, even if you haven't felt particularly brave or strong (*hint: that's often when we are being the bravest and the strongest*). And I trust that you are better able to answer grief when it comes knocking to ask if you know who you *really* are and who God *really* is.

This week, as we wrap up, we will revisit each of our five storm-guides. Yes, they each have a bit more to teach us.

Moses wrote Deuteronomy. Right at the beginning, he experienced a new grief.

Read Deuteronomy 3:23-29

What was the plea that Moses offered to God? (verse 25)

What was God's response? (verse 27)

Ouch. After being rescued from the water as a baby, after escaping to Midian, after being called back into his pain, after seeing all the gods of Egypt defeated, and after being brought out of Egypt once and for all, Moses never got to set foot on the Promised Land. Honestly, if I was writing the Book of Deuteronomy, I probably would have stopped there. But Moses didn't.

Moses was given a new command. What was it? (verse 28)

There's no doubt in my mind that this decision grieved Moses. Yet he now knew who he was, and he now knew who God was. So he dealt with this grief much differently than his first.

Write down one thing you've learned about grief that you want to carry into future griefs:

Moses continued to direct Israel towards God, preparing them for what was ahead, and reminding them of what was behind. **Because he was still free.** His faith in God wasn't dependent on getting into the Promised Land. I think ours is sometimes, if we're honest.

See, for some He offers and promises the Promised Land. But not to all. I can't count how many times I have heard people (good, loving, God-fearing but **no-idea-what-kind-of-awful-theology-they-be-preachin'-people**) say something like

> *"Well, as soon as you are okay with being single,*
> *God will bring you a husband."* Chuckle chuckle.

Or *"I'm SURE you'll get pregnant*
as soon as you stop trying." Wink wink.

> Or *"As soon as _____,*
> *I'm sure God will _____";*

As if God is a cosmic bully just waiting for you to get bored enough to stop wanting the toy before He will give it to you. Gross.

I mean, can you imagine if someone said, *"Oh Moses, I'm sure that as soon as you stop WANTING to go into the Promised Land, God will let you in."* Actually, I bet people did say that. I mean, humanity hasn't changed that much in six thousand years.

When we promise each other things that God didn't promise, we run smack-dab into bad theology. It happens all the time. Often accidentally. But accidents can be fatal. So I'm-a-just-sayin': be careful. If you've been handed some bad theology like this, write a reply here that's based on the truth of who God actually is:

Read Deuteronomy 6:10-13

How is God described in verse 12?

Note: I love that Moses still referred to God this way. He's still the God who brought them out of Egypt. Amidst his new grief, He didn't call Him "the God who is keeping me out of the Promised Land". Oh how much I have to learn from this man.

How is life described in verses 10-11?

What does it say they will NOT do in the land God is bringing them into?

These are all the things they once did for others, as if to stamp their new identity with an exclamation point: **YOU ARE NO LONGER SLAVES.**

What is the danger that Moses is warning against in verse 12?

What's the "Egypt" that God has brought you out of?
Or perhaps is bringing you out of even now?

What are some of the "good cities, full vineyards" in YOUR life "after Egypt"?
Maybe some you're experiencing now,
maybe some you're still looking forward to.

How can you "take care" not to forget God as the memory of Egypt fades?

Read Deuteronomy 8:17-18

What does Moses identify as the greatest lie we have to be careful against as our "wealth" is restored?

And what is the TRUTH to cling to as we "take care"? (verse 18)

Read Deuteronomy 11:1-7

In verses 3-4, what does Moses charge them to remember? *I know, it gets repetitive, right? Trust me, there are LOADS of verses I'm not having you read that say the same thing. Again. Me thinks it mattered to him.*

In verse 7, what does Moses give as a reason to love the Lord?

What have YOUR eyes seen of the great work of the Lord?

Read Exodus 16:2-12

What were the people of Israel grumbling to Moses about here?

So he was used to their grumbling. That's probably why he kept warning them against that in Deuteronomy. Again, us humans haven't changed that much in six thousand years.

What did they want to do? (verse 3)

Sometimes we may look back at Egypt – the place of our pain – and actually think that sounds comfortable. Crazy, but true.

"Going back to Egypt" can look like a lot of different things. It can be as simple as letting the label get the best of you, starting to believe it defines you, or being more comfortable as a victim. Pain can become a place to hide.

What does Moses say that God will do instead of letting them go back to Egypt?

Why does it say He will do that? (verse 12)

Sometimes even after we've left the place of pain and captivity, we need reminders that God is God. New things to hold to. Like bread falling from the sky. And so it did.

DON'T GO BACK TO EGYPT.
- God
No, seriously, don't.
There's nothing left there for you.

As a Scuba Diver, I'll never forget the most important rule my Instructor taught me – the one that trumped all others:
"Make the same number of ascents as descents."
The same is true for digging into pain.
We descend for a reason – to see something new.
But we are not made to live down there.

We must make the same
number of ascents as descents.

Egypt is used as a reference point throughout Israel's history, not only as a physical place but as a reference to a mindset of captivity, of fear. God repeatedly places prophets before the people saying "*Don't go back there. Trust me.*" Yet Egypt had this *draw*, like a magnet tugging them back.

Read Isaiah 31:1-5

What is the instruction in verse 1?

What is the comparison between God and Egypt in verse 3?

What does it say that God will do if they trust Him enough to NOT go back to Egypt? (verses 4-5)

Read Jeremiah 42:7-17

For *over 900 years* after God rescued Israel from Egypt, they kept wanting to go back. Before we chide, let's be honest about how often we do this. We've all seen the person who has taken up permanent residency in Egypt, in pain. We are scared to be that person. And I think we're scared of it because, in our most honest places, we know how easy it would be to return there. There's something about what we knew before that sounds, well, familiar, maybe even comfortable. But also, deadly.

In this passage, as the Chaldean army destroyed Jerusalem (yep, the same Chaldeans that Habakkuk is complaining about), some survivors went to Jeremiah and asked if they could go back to Egypt.
But they really had already made up their minds that that was the best option. They didn't really want God's answer.

In verses 10-12, what does God promise to them if they will dare to trust Him and stay in Jerusalem?

In verse 14, what things do they identify as reasons they would want to go back to Egypt?

In verses 15-17, what things does God say will find them if they run back to Egypt?

In Jeremiah 43, the people decide that Jeremiah is lying to them, and they decide to go back to Egypt, where destruction found them as promised.

You guys, once we've been rescued from Egypt, once we've been redeemed through our pain, WE ARE NOT TO GO BACK THERE TO LIVE. Ok then, good talk. Good talk.

Is there an "Egypt" that beckons to you?
Identify the reasons you are drawn back.

What is it that you need to trust God with in resisting a return to Egypt?

A prayer for today from a verse for today:

Read Deuteronomy 7:6-9

Fill in the blanks using this passage as a guide but inserting your name and redemption from your Egypt:

For _____(your name) is holy to the Lord God. The Lord God has chosen _____(your name) for his _____ possession, out of all the _____ on the face of the _____. It was not because _____(your name) is more valuable than any other _____ that the Lord set his _____ on _____(your name) and chose _____(your name), but it is because the Lord _____ _____(your name) and is keeping the oath that he swore to Israel, that the Lord has brought _____(your name) out of _____ (your Egypt) with a mighty hand and _____ _____(your name) from the house of that _____, from the hand of _____ (your Pharoahs). Know therefore that the Lord _____'s(your name) God is _____, the _____ God who keeps _____ and _____ love with those who love him and keep His commandments.

US – Day 2
From the Two and Martha: Unashamed of Hope

Jesus showed the Two on the Road how to find Him when they couldn't see Him. And in so doing, left us a roadmap *through His Word.*

Jesus showed Martha to hold onto hope even when common sense screams that dead people stink.

Still, it's not always easy to keep your hope alive in Someone we can't see (yet) and can't touch (yet).

Read Psalm 119:116

What is the prayer here?
The request expressed in the second half of the verse?

Those of us who have grieved know what it's like to hope. And what it feels like to desperately hold onto it. And what it's like to be ashamed to hold onto it.

Have you ever felt ashamed of hope? Describe.

We see here the same path that the Two were taken down.
How is our hope sustained according to this verse?

© Brooke Mardell, 2016, v 2

*Another translation of "your promise" is "your Word".

Read Isaiah 54

What are the instructions in verses 1, 2, and 4?

What things are the barren and the desolate specifically told to do?

Glance back at Isaiah 53. It's a passage of great grief. I don't think it's a coincidence that this chapter follows.

It was one of those particularly painful days – you know the ones, when your soul feels most fragile - that I came upon this instruction. To me, the barren one. *"Go enlarge your tents. Strengthen your stakes."* Wha???? I mean, it sounded kind of cruel. And confusing. Still, as I sat in my small, empty house, I asked God *"what does this even mean?"* And one baby step at a time (no pun intended), I looked at my "tents", the rooms in my heart. I looked to expand. I started opening my heart up to new things that my "tents" were available for since there was some empty space. I made more time for friendships. I signed up to be a counselor for a camp for foster youth. And my heart found healing as I came to know the names and faces of neglected and abused children.

And my "stakes", what were those? For me, my main stake, the thing that keeps me anchored, is my marriage. So I looked for ways to strengthen it. To invest in it. And oh what a payoff. My tents are now enlarged, my stakes are strong. Yes I remain barren, but I have a better idea of why I'm told to sing.

What are your tents?

What are ways you can enlarge them?

What are your stakes?

What are some ways you can strengthen them?

Strengthen your stakes.
Enlarge your tents.
Hope > Shame.

Look at verse 10. What is the Lord's promise to you?

Look at verses 11-17. How does verse 11 start out?
This is important because the promise that follows is specifically to this person:

Who is talking here as the "builder" of this beautiful, fortified city?

- 162 -

Friday's Rain   © Brooke Mardell, 2016, v.2

**It's not on our own strength that our tents will be enlarged
and our stakes will be strengthened.**

Read 1 Peter 1:3-9

What type of hope has been given to us through Christ's resurrection?

How is our inheritance described in verse 4?

Look at verses 8-9. What about these verses reminds you of the Two on the Road?

What is the outcome in verse 8? What do we get to feel?

And what is the outcome for our souls? (verse 9)

A prayer for today: your words to Him

Write out a prayer to the God who can be found when He can't be seen, and in whom our Hope has no reason for shame:

A verse for today: His words to you

I am not ashamed to be called your God.

- Hebrews 11:16

US – Day 3
From Peter: Choosing the Giver over the gift

In joining Peter on Friday, we saw a raw, honest man with a raw, honest heart. And while his grief was deep, there's another grief that took place in that same moment. There was another heart that broke as Peter wept bitterly. It's the same heart that broke every time that Israel turned away. Every time that His promises weren't believed. Every time that the gift was chosen over the Giver.

So when Peter and Jesus talked things out at the lakeshore, it wasn't only Peter's heart being mended.

Read Isaiah 53:3

How is the Messiah described?

It's not a stretch of the imagination to think that Peter's rejection was one of the reasons that Jesus was acquainted with grief.

Read Luke 1:78

How is God's mercy described?

Make no mistake. Tenderness is not weakness. We have a God who is at once fierce and tender. He is both the Lion and the Lamb (Rev. 5). I know, mystery-upon-mystery.

Still, all too often I think His strength and fierceness is emphasized at the sacrifice of His tender-heartedness. This isn't about wearing kid-gloves with God, but it is about realizing there is a depth of emotion, compassion, and yes grief that is expressed by God as He interacts with us, not just the other way around. The God of the Bible – especially of the Old Testament – often gets a bad rap as this impersonal, distant, harsh God. And then Jesus is the warm and fuzzy one. Not so. Both are fierce. Both are tender.

And there's this fascinating mystery unveiled when we realize that we are both, too. In learning about our own grief, we learn about God. In learning about His grief, we learn about ours. Why?

Read Genesis 1:27

Whose image does mankind reflect?

> There are no ordinary people.
> You have never talked to a mere mortal.
> Nations, cultures, arts, civilizations –
> these are mortal, and their life is
> to ours as the life of a gnat.
> But it is immortals whom we joke with,
> work with, marry, snub and exploit –
> immortal horrors or everlasting splendors.
>
> - C.S. Lewis,
> - *The Weight of Glory*

Take a close look at some of your deepest feels.

I'm talking about the ones that you feel without telling yourself to. Look at some of those pieces of your heart, both those of joy and those of pain. What do they teach you about GOD's heart?

For example:

It hurts that I can't make a baby	→	I am made in the image of a life-maker
this part of my heart	*shows me*	*this part of God's heart*

I love discovering new places u	→	I am made in the image of an adventurer
this part of my heart	*shows me*	*this part of God's heart*

Your turn:

_____   →   _____
this part of my heart   *shows me*   *this part of God's heart*

_____   →   _____
this part of my heart   *shows me*   *this part of God's heart*

← The next time you feel something deep within you
– be it of joy or pain – ask God this question:
"*what does this teach me about YOU?*
What about this feeling is a hint about the image of yours that I bear?" →

Read Exodus 33:1-3
When I read this, I hear a God who is grieving loss.
What does He say the people will still receive?

What does he say they will NOT receive?

Read Exodus 33:12-17

What does Moses beg God for?

Moses is not satisfied with what God will give him – he wants HIM. This is so reminiscent to me of Jesus' talk with Peter. Gifts aside, do you want ME, the giver?

Confession time. I was a scared new bride. No, not of THAT. Okay, a little of that.
But I was scared that I loved him "too much." I was afraid that God would take him from me.
What an ugly picture of my beautiful God. But seriously, I would play Goldilocks and
try to love him not too little and not too much but *"juuuust ricggght"*, so that God
would be pleased but not jealous.

About three years into our marriage, God called me out on this.
And showed me that by trying to walk this tight-rope, by living
in this fear, I was missing the fullness of both the gift AND
the Giver. That in fact one way to love Him as the Giver
was to love this gift He had given me and not hold back.

Identify a "gift" in your life that has competed with the Giver? That you're
tempted to be satisfied in ...

Take a minute and thank the Giver for that gift. Because this isn't about self-
martyrdom and not enjoying good gifts. He gives good gifts (James 1:17). I
mean, He made puppies, you guys.

- 168 -

Read Isaiah 63:8-10

When Israel rebelled, what did it do to God's Spirit?

Okay a tough question. Well, really, a tough answer. Pause and ask God what is in your life, thoughts, actions right now that could be grieving Him? Write down anything He shows you:

Read Psalm 103:8-13

Write down how these verses describe how God responds to you:

Take these to heart. He means it.

Read Jeremiah 31:31-34

How does God describe what HE is looking forward to in the new covenant?
*Remember, we are living under the new covenant.

Read Ephesians 2:19-22

What is the transformation described? From foreigners and aliens to what? What does that tell you about how God sees you?

Read John 14:1-3

What does Jesus describe about His father's house?

What does He say He and the Father are doing?

Who is it being prepared for?

Don't look now, but I dare say that God doesn't just love us, but LIKES us.

Read Ephesians 4:30

What is asked of us here?

In light of a God who likes you, wants to live with you, who craves relationship with you, who can get angry but who does so slowly ... what does it mean to you when He says "don't grieve me"? What does it reveal to you about Him?

Read Revelation 21:1-7

This is the description of what is yet to come. Write down what GOD is looking forward to about it:

Until then, He's doing something rather beautiful with our griefs.

Read Psalm 56:8

What is God doing with your tears?

I mean, *hello tender.* Only someone who loves you, likes you, and GETS YOU could do that. Take some time to reflect on these precious pictures that God paints of His heart towards us. Ponder what it means to believe that God really likes you, and that He is a God who has a heart that can be broken. And then remember that You are created in His image. **With all the feels.**

A prayer for today: your words to Him

A verse for today: His words to you

Pick one from what you read today and write it out here:

Habakkuk taught me how to praise God without any answers. His final prayer in Habakkuk 3:17-19 has continued to resonate with me for years. I guess you could say he was my first true picture of what contentment looks like. Because he never said he LIKED what was happening, just that he would trust God in it.

Being discontent is a way of saying "I don't believe God is in this."
- Darin McWatters

Gah, another sermon on contentment. I've always translated "contentment" as a way of saying "I'm okay with this", or even complacency. All throughout the sermon, part of me was raging against what I'm not ready to "endorse". But I'd never thought of DISCONTENT as a way of saying You're not in something.

How many times have I just "postponed the discontent" instead of walking through both good and bad coming from You?

January 31, 2011

Have you ever "postponed" discontentment? Kept busy while you waited for things to change? Before studying Habakkuk in this way, what I called contentment was really just postponing discontentment – pasting on smiles and telling myself everything was fine even while me heart gnawed on *that thing*. Describe one of those times here.

Habakkuk showed us what it meant to look into the discontent. To find out what was really nagging at us. Describe what you've found as you've looked into your discontent.

One of the most famous passages about contentment was penned by Paul, a man who lived in prisons and through shipwrecks and who went from murderous fiend to zealous friend of the Church overnight. So, you know, he lived a little.

Read Philippians 4:10-13

What circumstances does Paul identify in verse12?

Paul speaks of himself as a student of his circumstances rather than a victim of them. What would it look like in your life to be a STUDENT of your circumstances? Imagine your circumstances as a teacher in front of you. And imagine yourself in third grade. Because just about everyone was cute in third grade. And eager to learn. What's on the chalkboard? What lessons are your circumstances teaching you right now?

Read verse 13 closely. It is often quoted as a stand-alone. Almost like an endorsement of "I can do whatever I want" ... I mean, I've heard it used about diets, studying, and leaping tall buildings. But look at what comes just before it. Paul says there's a "secret" in verse 12. What is the secret?

← What if verse 13 was the answer to the secret? The secret ingredient to what verse 12 offers →

If discontent is saying I do NOT see God in this, then TRUE contentment is saying I will watch for my God in all things.

Read Hebrews 13:5-6

WHY are we told to be content with what we have?

What can we be confident about saying?

Contentment = seeing WHO is there.
Discontent = seeing WHAT is not.

Read Psalm 23. Yep, again.

What comes right before "Even though I walk through the valley of the shadow of death"? Write out the sentence that precedes it.

What if the two are connected? What if the path of righteousness sometimes leads us into the valley for his name's sake? Does that shed new light on your path today? If so, share.

In verse 4, he says he will feel no fear. Why? Who is with him in the presence of his enemies?

Where shall he dwell?

We see the Shepherd who leads, guides and restores become more and more active, more and more present, and more and more personal as this Psalm progresses. We see the Psalmist build the emphasis on God's presence and ultimately land on getting to live with Him forever as his highest value.

Read Revelation 21:3

How is the dwelling place of God described?

Read 2 Corinthians 6:16

Where will God make his dwelling?

If God wrote Hallmark cards,
I'm pretty sure they'd all say something like
*"My favorite place
in the whole world - in all of time –
is WITH YOU."*

The God of the Bible reveals Himself as WITH US. In all things. His presence is our secret ingredient, our secret weapon, in finding true contentment. In all things.

A prayer for today: your words to Him

Write a prayer inviting God to show You where He is
in your circumstances, and how, through Him, you can be content .
Trust me, I *know* how hard this prayer can be.
Remember, this isn't about who we are, but who He is.

A verse for today: His words to you

I have been your help ... I will uphold you by my right hand.
- Psalm 63:7a, 8b

US – Day 5
Revealing the beauty of the
Beloved and the Belover

I don't like grief. I don't like pain. I'm not the girl who signs up for the gym because it-hurts-so-good. Also, I don't sign up for the gym for any other reason. I didn't write this Study so that we could cozy up and make nice with our griefs, but so that we could stare them down and see what we had to GAIN in the midst of LOSS.

> Grief is not the boss of me.
> - Us

Still, grief, pain and loss are real. And for most of us, life isn't short enough for one major grief. While infertility was my First Great Grief. As you've seen, it certainly wasn't my last. Even as I write this I am trying to wrap my head around a new diagnosis of someone I love. **There's a new storm-a-brewin'**. A new place of pain to find my God in. For Him to Redeem. But see, now I've got the storm gear. Now I know that loss doesn't have the last word. I know who's with me *in* the rain, not just after the rainbow.

So as you reflect back, summarize the storm you have walked/are walking through – these answers may still be fuzzy, or perhaps crystal clear. Both are okay.

What's the *lightning strike* that's rocked your world?

What is God asking you in the rumble of the *thunder*?

What is the first step in responding and what *storm gear* do you need?

What part of the path *through* the storm can you see right now?

What is being revealed to you in the *cloudbreak?*

The other night we were driving through fog. Dense, thick fog. The kind that looks like soup. No matter that this is a road I've been on over a thousand times. No matter that I can predict most of it's twists and turns as it climbs the mountain. The clouds change everything. Flashers on. Speed slowed. Eyes focused. Because the thing you've done a thousand times is different when you're doing it in the middle of a cloud. It requires about eight thousand times more effort to just see the yellow line and not veer off the cliff.And then, the clouds lifted. The clarity of the sky was all the more obvious as our eyes relaxed and shoulders un-tensed. We were through it. Through the worst of the storm.

That's how the grief-storm can feel too.
Like the things you've done a thousand times before now
require a new focus and energy. But the clouds are not forever.
They will break.

Read Isaiah 43:1-7

Write out the promises you see here:

Read Ecclesiastes 3:1-14

List the things "there is a time" for:

Circle the ones that you are allowing "a time for" right now.
Draw a box around the ones you want to give time to.

For those you've drawn a circle around, identify what it looks like to give time to that:

For those you've drawn a box around, identify the things you need to do to make time available:

Read Jeremiah 31

Write down the passage(s) that stand out to you. These are God's gift to you today:

Loss doesn't have the last word.
- God

WEEK 6 REFLECTION
YOUR PSALM

The Psalms are made of proclamations and realizations about who God is and who we are. They are God's truths meeting His people in their deepest moments. They are filled with praise, questions, and commitments.

You've been writing a Psalm throughout this Study. Now it's time to put it together. A series of your own proclamations and realizations. Go back through Weeks 1-5 and gather the declarations you made at the end of each week; re-write them here:

Because God is _____

I know that I am _____

Because God is _____

I know that I am _____

Because God is _____

I know that I am _____

Because God is _____

I know that I am _____

Because God is _____

I know that I am _____

We are deeply loved, by a wild Belover. The sacredness of loss is being able to find our truest selves and our truest God in the deep places. Thank you for going deep, for braving the storm, and for daring to search for the Sacred in the Sad. I trust that He found you in your pursuit. Loss so does not have the last word.

So as your story continues, I'd love nothing more than to hear about it. You can reach me at www.brookemardell.com

Until then,

brookemardell

CPSIA information can be obtained
at www.ICGtesting.com
Printed in the USA
FSOW02n0629070416
18912FS